THE HOLY QUR'AN AND THE SCIENCES OF NATURE

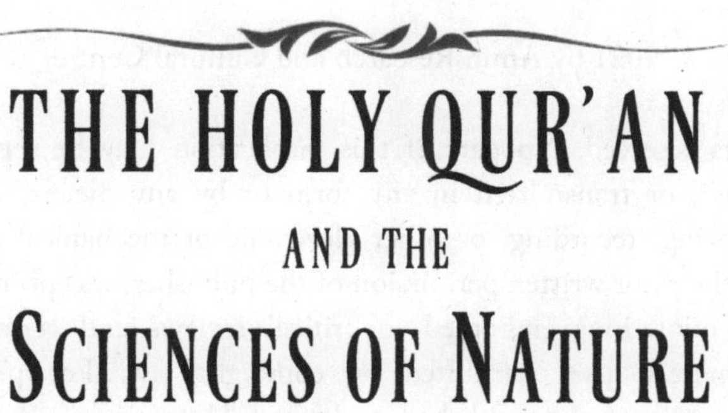

THE HOLY QUR'AN AND THE SCIENCES OF NATURE

Mehdi Golshani

Professor of Physics
Sharif University of Technology, Tehran, Iran

Ordering Information:
Quantity sales. Special discounts are available on quantity purchases by corporations, associations, and others. For details, contact the distributor at the address below.

Shia Books Australia
www.shiabooks.com.au
info@shiabooks.com.au

ISBN 978-967-10379-1-1

Third Edition 2021

Title: THE HOLY QUR'AN AND THE SCIENCE OF NATURE
Author: PROF. MEHDI GOLSHANI

ISBN 978-967-10379-1-1

First published 2008
Institute for Humanities and Culture Studies (IHCS)
Tehran, Iran

This Revised Edition 2011 by
Amin Research and Cultural Centre (ARCC)
No. 314, Jalan 4, Taman Ampang Utama
68000 Selangor Darul Ehsan
Tel: +603 4257 3080

Printed by
Academe Art & Printing Services
Kuala Lumpur

Contetns

PREFACE 1

I. SCIENCE AND THE MUSLIM UMMAH

Introduction 3

Sciences Whose Knowledge Is *Wājib Kifā'ī* 7

Category of *Wājib Kifā'ī* Sciences 9

Necessity of Learning Other Sciences 13

Criterion for the Usefulness of Any Science 24

Decline of Sciences in the Islamic World 30

Proposals 33

II. THE SIGNIFICANCE OF PHYSICAL AND BIOLOGICAL SCIENCES IN ISLAMIC PERSPECTIVE

Introduction 36

Islam and Science 42

1. The Role of Science in Knowing God 42
2. The Role of Science in the Advancement of an Islamic Society 55

Conclusion 63

III. SCIENCE AND ETHICS IN THE QUR'ANIC OUTLOOK

Moral Dimension of Human Beings in the Qur'anic Outlook 72

Moral Dimension of Science and Technology 76

Science and Ethics in the Contemporary World 79

IV. FROM KNOWLEDGE TO WISDOM: A QUR'ANIC PERSPECTIVE

Introduction 81

The Need for the Integration of Knowledge with Wisdom 82

Wisdom in the Islamic Perspective 84

Why Wisdom Is Absent in Our Era? 86

Conclusion 91

V. SCIENTIFIC DIMENSION OF THE QUR'AN

The Qur'an as a Source of Scientific Knowledge 93

The Qur'an as a Book of Guidance 99

Our View 101

Qur'an Message for Muslim Scientists 103

VI. PHILOSOPHY OF SCIENCE: A QUR'ANIC APPROACH

The Aim of Understanding Nature 108

The Possibility of Understanding Nature 110

The Main Issues in Understanding Nature 112

Ways of Understanding Nature 119

Stages in Understanding Nature 153

Impediments of Cognition 171

Guiding Principles in Understanding Nature 195

INDEX OF NAMES 227

END NOTES 231

Preface

The study of the Qur'anic view concerning the cognition of nature has a long history in the Islamic world. In the golden era of Islamic civilization, most of the learned Muslim scholars considered the Qur'an as the source of their inspiration in their study of nature, and they viewed the discovery of the secrets of nature as a way for their familiarity with the signs of Allah in natural world and an effective way for proximity to Allah.

The rise of modern science and its rapid development was after the decadence of the sciences of nature in the Islamic world. When, about two centuries ago, Muslims started to import Western science, several attitudes developed in the Islamic world. Some scholars saw modern science as the only key to their future development and discarded the Qur'an completely. On the other hand, some scholars saw the root of all sciences in the Holy Qur'an and tried to adapt the Holy Qur'an with findings of modern science. Finally, some eminent Muslim scholars, viewed the Holy Qur'an as the source of their worldview and inspiration in the discovery of nature, but they also recommended the use of the methods and tools of modern science .This writer belongs to the last category.

This book contains several essays which were first presented at some international conferences, but are now ordered in a logical order. These essays deal with different aspects of the relation of the sciences of nature with the Holy Qur'an, among which are the following subjects:

- the Islamic conception of knowledge;
- the reason for the significance of the sciences of nature from the Qur'anic viewpoint;
- the necessity of binding science with moral values;
- the necessity of binding science with wisdom;
- epistemology from the Qur'anic viewpoint.

In my humble view, the neglect of the Qur'anic worldview has deprived many Muslim scholars from the comprehensive inspirations of the Qur'an concerning the study of the natural world. I hope and pray that this humble presentation would work as a small spark in attracting Muslim scholars' attention to this comprehensive world view, in the revival of scientific spirit in the '*Ummah*, and in promoting scientific knowledge in the Muslim world.

The English edition of this book was published in New York twice. Then the expanded edition was published by the Institute for Humanities and Cultural Studies, Tehran, Iran. Now that the last edition is being republished by Amin Research and Cultural Centre (ARCC) of Malaysia, I would like to thank Mr. Ramin Ghavifekr of this center's publication department for his effort in publishing this book, and Mr. Mohamad Mohideen Jalaluddin for the typesetting of the book.

Mehdi Golshani

29 September 2011, Tehran, Iran

I

Science and the Muslim Ummah

Introduction

One of the distinctive features of Islam is its emphasis on knowledge. The Qur'an and the Islamic tradition (*sunnah*) invite Muslims to seek and acquire knowledge and wisdom and to hold men of knowledge in high esteem. Some of the Qur'anic verses and relevant traditions will be mentioned in the course of our discussion.

At the outset we may recall a famous *hadith* of the Holy Prophet (upon whom be Allah's peace and benedictions) that has come down through various sources; it says:

﴿طلب العلم فريضة علي كل مسلم.﴾

"Acquisition of knowledge is incumbent on every Muslim." [1]

This tradition brought up the discussion as to what kind of knowledge a Muslim should necessarily acquire an issue around which various opinions were offered in the past.

Abu Hamid Al-Ghazzali (died A.D. 1111), in his famous book *Ihyā 'Ulūm al-Dīn* (The Revival of Religious Sciences), mentions that he had come across twenty different answers to the above question.[2] The theologians considered that learning of Islamic theology (*kalām*) was an obligation, while the jurisprudents (*fuqahā*) thought that Islamic jurisprudence (*fiqh*) was implied in the prophetic tradition. Al-Ghazzali himself favoured the view that the knowledge whose acquisition is a religious obligation is limited to what one must know for correct performance of the acts obligatory for a person within the framework of the Islamic *Shari'ah.*[3] For instance, one whose occupation is animal husbandry should acquaint himself with the rules concerning *zakāt.* If one were a merchant doing business in an usurious environment, he ought to be aware of the religious injunction against usury so as to be able to effectively avoid it.

Al-Ghazzali then proceeds to discuss sciences whose knowledge is *wājib kifā'ī*[4] (something which is obligatory for the whole society as long as the duty for fulfillment of a social need exists, but as soon as the duty is shouldered by enough number of individuals, others are automatically relieved of the obligation). Subsequently, he classifies all knowledge into "religious" and "non-religious" sciences. By "religious sciences" (*'ulum al-shar'*) he means the bulk of knowledge imparted through prophetic teachings and the Revelation. The rest constitute the "non-religious" sciences. The non-religious sciences are further classified into "praiseworthy" (*mahmud*), "permissible" (*mubah*) and "undesirable" ones (*madhmum*). He puts history in the category of permissible sciences (*mubah*) and magic and sorcery in the category of the undesirable fields of "knowledge". The "praiseworthy" sciences (*mahmud*), according to him, are those whose knowledge is necessary in the affairs of life and these are *wājib kifā'ī*; the rest of them bring additional merit to the learned who pursue them. He puts medicine, mathematics and crafts, whose sufficient knowledge is needed by the society, in the category of sciences which are *wājib kifā'ī.* Any further research into the detail and depth of problems of medical sciences or mathematics is put by Al-Ghazzali in the second category which involves merit for the scholar without entailing any manner of obligation.

Al-Ghazzali classifies the religious sciences also into two groups: praiseworthy (*mahmud*) and undesirable (*madhmum*). By "undesirable religious sciences" he means those which are apparently oriented towards the *Shari'ah* but actually deviate from its teachings. He subdivides the "praiseworthy" religious sciences into four groups:

1. *Usul* (principles; i.e. the Qur'an, the *sunnah, ijmā' or* consensus and the traditions of the Prophet's companions)
2. *Furū'* (secondary matters; i.e. problems of jurisprudence, ethics and mystical experience)
3. Introductory studies (Arabic grammar, syntax, etc.)
4. Complementary studies (recitation and interpretation of the Qur'an, study of the principles of jurisprudence, *'ilm al-rijāl* or biographical research about narrators of Islamic traditions etc.)

Al-Ghazzali considers the knowledge of the disciplines contained in the above four groups to be *wājib kifā'ī.*

As to the extent to which one should learn the "praiseworthy" sciences, Al-Ghazzali's view is that in matters of theology such as knowledge of God, Divine qualities, acts and commands, one should try to learn as much as is possible. However, as to religious topics whose knowledge is *wājib kifā'ī*, one should learn as much as is sufficient. Here the summary of his views is that one should not pursue learning of those sciences if there are already others devoting themselves to their study, and if one were to do so, he should refrain from spending all his life for their learning, "for knowledge is vast and life is short. They are preliminaries and not an end in themselves."[5]

As to theology (*kalām*), his opinion is that only as much of it as is corroborated by the Qur'an and *hadith is* beneficial. Moreover, he says, "now that the heretics attempt to induce doubts (in the minds of unsophisticated believers), adequate knowledge of theology is necessary to confront them."

Regarding philosophy, Al-Ghazzali thinks that it is distinguishable into four parts: [6]

1. Mathematics and geometry, which are legitimate and permissible.
2. Logic, which is a part of theology.
3. Divinities, which discusses Divine essence and qualities and is also a part of theology.
4. Physics, which may be divided into two sections: One part which involves discussions opposed to the *Shari'ah* and accordingly cannot even be considered a "science"; the other part discusses the qualities of bodies. The second part is similar to the science of medicine, although medicine is preferable to it. This section of physics is useless while medicine is needful.

Mulla Muhsin Fayd al-Kashani, in his book *Muhajjat al-Baydā,* says:

It is a personal obligation (wājib 'aynī) of every Muslim to learn Islamic jurisprudence to the extent of his needs. Further, learning of fiqh to fulfill the need of others is wājib kifā'ī for him. [7]

Regarding philosophy, Kashani says:

The components of philosophy are not the only ones distinguished by Abu Hamid [Al-Ghazzali]–upon whom be God's mercy. Philosophy covers many other fields of religious and mundane matters (for example astronomy, medicine and rhetoric etc.)... Whatever of these sciences that is about the Hereafter exists to the point of perfection in the Shari'ah, and that which is not useful for the Hereafter is not needed; moreover, it may even hinder the pursuit of the path of Allah. In the case of those portions which are effective for the knowledge of the Divine and are encouraged by the Shari'ah (like astronomy), it is sufficient to be satisfied with the simple unelaborated discussions of the Shari'ah about such matters. [8]

In brief, in Kashani's opinion anyone who wishes to learn these sciences should first acquaint himself with the religious sciences.

Sadr al-Din Shirazi (Mulla Sadra) in his commentary on *Usul al-Kafi* regards Al-Ghazzali's opinion about the limitation of obligatory knowledge for a Muslim to the matters of ritual practice and legitimate dealings as unacceptable.[9] In his opinion, learning of religious sciences (such as *tawhid,* Divine qualities and acts) and human sciences (such as dispositions of the soul, its delights and afflictions) are also obligatory for the majority of human beings. Secondly, he believes that it is not at all essential that what is obligatory (*wājib 'aynī*) for all to learn should apply identically in case of every individual and what is obligatory for one individual be regarded as being equally obligatory for another.

Sciences Whose Knowledge Is Wājib Kifā'ī

Here we do not intend to enter into a discussion about sciences whose learning is obligatory (*wājib 'aynī*) for every responsible Muslim individual (*mukallaf*). Rather, we propose to discuss those sciences whose knowledge is a *wājib kifā'ī* for all the Muslim Ummah. To begin with, we consider some of the opinions of Imam Al-Ghazzali and Muhaqqiq Kashani in this regard as disputable and shall proceed to examine them. However, before we do that, we think it will be beneficial to revert to certain important points mentioned by Mulla Sadra in his commentary on *Usūl al-Kāfī* under the tradition:

﴿طلب العلم فريضة علي كل مسلم.﴾

Acquisition of knowledge is an obligation of every Muslim.

1. The word *'ilm* (knowledge or science), like the word "existence" (*wujūd*) has a broad range of meanings which vary from the viewpoints of strength or weakness, perfection or deficiency.[10]

The word's generic sense covers this whole spectrum of meanings in which it has been used in the prophetic tradition. This broad sense of the word *'ilm is* common to all of its varied meanings. Accordingly, the tradition intends to state that whatever stage of knowledge one may be in, he should strive to make further advance. The Prophet meant that acquisition of knowledge is obligatory for all Muslims, scholars as well as ignorant men, beginners as well as learned scholars. Whatever stage of knowledge man may attain, he is still like a child entering into adulthood as far as this tradition is concerned; i.e. he should learn things which were not obligatory for him before.

2. The tradition implies that a Muslim can never be relieved of his responsibility of acquiring knowledge.[11]

3. No field of knowledge or science is undesirable or detestable in itself; for knowledge is like light and so it is always desirable. The reason that some of the sciences have been regarded as "undesirable" is because of their occasional misuse.[12]

We do not accept the division of knowledge into "religious" and "non-religious" sciences; for, as Murtadā Mutahharī rightly pointed out, this classification may bring about the misunderstanding that the "non-religious" sciences are alien to Islam. This is not compatible with the comprehensive unity held up by Islam in all affairs of life. A religion which claims the ability to bring about conditions for perfect felicity of mankind and considers itself to be self-sufficing cannot estrange itself from things which play a vital role in the provision of welfare and independence for an Islamic society. According to the late Mutahhari:

> *"Islam's all-inclusiveness and finality as a religion demands that every field of knowledge that is beneficial for an Islamic society be regarded as a part and parcel of the "religious sciences."*[13]

Category of Wājib Kifā'ī Sciences

We think that the group of sciences belonging to the category of *wājib kifā'ī is* much larger than what Al-Ghazzali would have us believe. Moreover, we think that the parsimony he shows regarding those sciences which may be included in this category, does not harmonize with the teachings of the Qur'an and the Prophet's *sunnah*. Our reasons for not accepting such restrictions on learning are as follows:

1. In most of the Qur'anic verses and traditions, the concept of *'ilm* (knowledge) appears in its absolutely general sense, as can be seen from examples given below:

﴿قل هل يستوي الذين يعلمون والذين لا يعلمون﴾ (الزمر/ 9)

"Say: Are those who know and those who do not know alike?"

(Sūrah 39:9)

﴿علّم الانسان ما لم يعلم﴾ (العلق/ 5)

"(God) taught man what he knew not."

(Sūrah 96:5)

﴿و علم آدم الاسماء كلها ثم عرضهم علي الملائكة فقال انبئوني باسماء هؤلاء ان كنتم صادقين﴾ (البقرة/ 31)

And He taught Adam all the names; then showed them to the angels, saying: "Tell me the names of these, if you are right."

(Sūrah 2:31)

2. Some Qur'anic verses and traditions confirm that knowledge does not mean only learning of the principles and laws of the *Shari'ah*. We may note some examples:

﴿و لقد آتينا داود و سليمان علماً و قالا الحمدلله الذي فضّلنا علي كثير من عباده المؤمنين و ورث سليمان داود و قال يا ايها الناس علّمنا منطق الطير و اوتينا من كل شيئ انّ هذا لهو الفضل المبين﴾ (النمل/ 16-15)

"And certainly We gave knowledge to David and Solomon, and both (the apostles) said: 'All praise is God's who made us to excel many of His believing servants. And Solomon succeeded David and he said: 'O people! We have been taught the language of the birds, and we have been granted (plenty) of everything; surely, this is manifest grace (of God)'."

(Sūrah 27: 15-16)

We see that the two prophets David and Solomon consider the knowledge of the language of birds to be a Divine blessing.

﴿الم تر انّ الله انزل من السماء ماءً فاخرجنا به ثمرات مختلفاً الوانه و من الجبال جدد بيض و حمر مختلف الوانها و غرابيب سود و من الناس والدواب والانعام مختلف الوانه كذلك انّما يخشيالله من عباده العلماء ...﴾ (فاطر/ 28-27)

"Do you not see that God sends down water from the shy, then We bring forth with it fruits of various colours, and in the mountains are streaks, white and red and of various colours and others intensely black? And of men and beasts and cattle are of various colours likewise; only those of His servants endowed with knowledge fear God ..."

(Sūrah 35:27-28)

Clearly, the phrase 'only those of his servants endowed with knowledge' occurring in the above verse refers to those who are aware of the laws and mysteries of nature and creation, and who acknowledge in all humility the greatness and majesty of God. The following traditions of the Prophet ﷺ also point to the most general sense of the word "knowledge".

﴿اطلبوا العلم ولو بالصّين، فانّ طلب العلم فريضة علي كل مسلم﴾

"Seek knowledge by even going to China, for seeking knowledge is incumbent on every Muslim." [14]

﴿اعلم الناس من جمع علم الناس الي علمه﴾

"The most learned of men is one who collects bits of knowledge from others and thus enhances his own knowledge." [15]

﴿من اراد الدنيا فعليه بالعلم و من اراد الآخرة فعليه بالعلم و من ارادهما معاً فعليه بالعلم﴾

"Anyone who desires the good of present life should seek knowledge. Anyone who desires the life of Hereafter should seek knowledge. And anyone who wants to do well in this life and in the next world should seek knowledge." [16]

﴿الحكمة ضالة المؤمن فحيث وجدها فهواحق بها﴾

"Wisdom is the believer's lost property, wherever he finds it, he deserves more than others to have it." [17]

From these sayings of the great Prophet of Islam and similar traditions, the truth emerges that such recommendations for acquisition of knowledge are not confined to the knowledge of the principles and laws of the *Shari'ah;* because, as is obvious, China was not a centre of theological studies in those days but was famous for its crafts and industry. Moreover, it is clear that the laws of *Shari'ah* and Islamic doctrines cannot be learnt from polytheists and infidels.

3. Another reason for not considering "desirable" knowledge to be limited to the religious and theological studies is the precious

heritage left by the Muslim scholars of the first several centuries of Islamic civilization. As is also confirmed by modern historians of science, Muslim scholars were at the vanguard of the scientific tradition for centuries and their books were used as text-books in Europe for several hundred years.

In fact the major reason why Muslim scholars did not reject the intellectual traditions of other countries was that they did not see any separation between the goal of religion and the ends of knowledge and were convinced that both religion and knowledge were aimed at illuminating the unity of nature and consequently the oneness of the Creator. Accordingly, it was on the basis of this conviction of intrinsic fusion of religion and knowledge that religious coaching and rational training were considered as aspects of a single discipline in religious schools and mosques.

4. To set aside a group of sciences on the pretext that they do not have as much value as the religious studies is not correct. Because, whatever field of knowledge is conductive to preservation of the strength and vitality of an Islamic society, its knowledge is *wājib kifā'ī* for the Islamic society in the same fashion as scholarship in religious sciences are, as has been pointed out in the following verse of the Qur'an:

﴿و ما كان المؤمنون لينفروا كافة فلولا نفر من كل فرقة منهم طائفة ليتفقهوا

في الدين ولينذروا قومهم اذا رجعوا اليهم لعلهم يحذرون﴾ (التوبة/ 122)

"It is not for the believers to go forth totally (to acquire scholarship in religion); but why should not a party of every section of them go forth, to become learned in religion, and to warn their people when they return to them, that haply they may beware?"

(Sūrah 9:122)

Thus, we may conclude that the word 'ilm' as it occurs in the Qur'an and *sunnah*, appears in a more general sense than the religious studies. On this ground it can be said that Islam has only dissuaded Muslims from preoccupying themselves with those branches of knowledge whose harm is greater than their benefit (like magic and sorcery and games of chance used for gambling). The relevant sayings of the Prophet ﷺ may be noted:

﴿خير العلم ما نفع﴾

"The best fields of knowledge are those which bring benefit."[18]

﴿اللّهم انفعني بما علّمتني و علّمني ما ينفعني وزدني علماً﴾

"O God! Benefit me from knowledge that You have bestowed on me, teach me whatever would benefit me, and increase my knowledge."[19]

Imam 'Alī (A) is related as having said:

﴿لا خير في علم لاينفع﴾

"There is no good in knowledge which does not benefit."[20]

﴿العلم اكثر من ان يحاط به، فخذوا من كل علم أحسنه﴾

"Knowledge is too immense in scope for anyone to be able to contain it. So learn from each science its best parts."[21]

Necessity of Learning Other Sciences

There is no division of opinion on the necessity of acquiring knowledge particular to religious studies. Accordingly, we shall abstain from any further discussion of the subject.[22] Instead, it is worthwhile to concentrate on the question of necessity of learning other sciences in the view of the

Qur'an and *sunnah. In* this regard there are a number of arguments which we present here.

1. If knowledge of a science is a preliminary requirement for attaining an Islamic goal, as envisaged by the *Shari ah,* its pursuit is an obligation (*wājib*), since it entails the preliminary condition for fulfillment of a duty prescribed by the *Shari'ah.* For example, the physical welfare of individuals in an Islamic society is necessary, hence it is a *wājib kifā'ī* for the Muslims to study medicine.

   Some are of the opinion that in this context the duty to learn any specific science depends on the need of the society for it. For example, in our day, in order to succeed in large-scale agriculture or commerce, specialized knowledge of these subjects is necessary. Accordingly, it is a *wājib kifā'ī* for Muslims to acquire specialty in these fields.

   Evidently, if the Muslims restrict themselves to the religious sciences and limit themselves to a minimum of what is necessary for their survival, they can never hope to catch or overtake the non-Muslim world *in* its scientific progress.

2. The society envisioned by the Qur'an is an independent society of majesty and grandeur, not one subservient to and dependent on the unbelievers, as can be seen from this verse of the Qur'an:

   ﴿... ولن يجعل الله للكافرين علي المؤمنين سبيلاً﴾ (النساء/ 141)

   "...and Allah does not grant the unbelievers any way (of domination) over the believers."

   (Sūrah 4: 141)

   In order to realize this goal set by the Qur'an, it is essential that the Islamic society should have cultural, political and economic independence; this in turn necessitates training of specialists of high caliber in every field and the creation of the necessary scientific and technical facilities in Islamic societies. It is clear that one of the reasons of decline of Muslim societies in the recent centuries is that they left the study of those sciences to others which they themselves deserved to study most; thus, they made themselves dependent on others. Should not the Muslims equip themselves in every way to defend themselves against the non-believers as stressed by the following verse?

﴿و اعدّوا لهم ما استطعتم من قوة و من رباط الخيل ترهبون به عدوّالله و عدوّكم ...﴾ (الانعام/ 60)

"And prepare against them whatever force you can ... so that you may dismay the enemy of God and your enemy ..."

(Sūrah 8:60)

Is it not true that in our world today, the possession of defence facilities to face the enemies of Islam requires all kinds of scientific and technical know-how? Then, why don't the Muslims give the necessary attention to the issue of preparing themselves adequately for their self-defence?

In the modern age, human life is inextricably linked with the effort for scientific advancement and the key to success in all affairs lies in knowledge. Thus, it is an obligation for Muslim scholars and researchers, living in the countries of the Eastern or Western block and engaged in education, to acquire the latest and most complete scientific and technical knowledge. Otherwise, their societies will inevitably remain under the domination of one superpower or another. Imam Ja'far al-Sādiq (A) says:

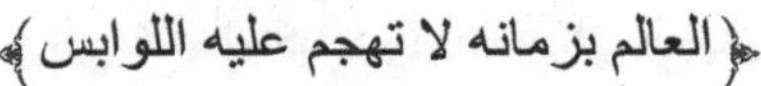

"A knowledgeable man who is abreast of his time will not be overwhelmed by unexpected problems." [23]

To sum up, if Muslims want to succeed in their struggle against the evil powers of their age, they should equip themselves with the essentials of scientific advancement and should try to make up their lag in scientific and technical fields. Thus, whatever subject is essential for safeguarding the existence and vitality of the Islamic societies should be learnt.

3. The Holy Qur'an invites mankind to study the system and scheme of creation, the wonders of nature and the causes and effects of all things that exist, the conditions of living organisms, and in short all signs of God discernable in the external universe and in the inner depths of the human soul. The Qur'an enjoins thought and meditation about all aspects of creation and requires human beings to apply their reason and perceptual faculties for the discovery of the secrets of nature. Here we quote a few of these verses:

﴿اولم تنظروا الي السماء فوقهم كيف بنيناها و زيّناها و ما لها من فروج والارض مددناها و القينا فيها رواسي و انبتنا فيها من كل زوج بهيج تبصرة و ذكري لكل عبد منيب﴾(ق/ 8-6)

"What, have they not beheld heaven above them, how We have built it, and decked it out fair, and it has no cracks? And the earth–We stretched it forth, and cast on it firm mountains, and We caused to grow therein of every joyous kind for an insight and a reminder to every penitent servant."

(Sūrah 50:6-8)

﴿افلا ينظرون الي الابل كيف خلقت و الي السماء كيف رفعت و الي الجبال كيف نصبت و الي الارض كيف سطحت﴾ (الغاشية/ 20-17)

"What do they not consider how the camel was created, how heaven was lifted up, how the mountains were hoisted, how the earth was outstretched?"

(Sūrah 88:17-20)

﴿قل سيروا في الارض فانظروا كيف بدء الخلق...﴾ (العنكبوت/ 20)

"Say: Journey in the land, then behold how He originated creation..."

(Sūrah 29:20)

﴿و في الارض آيات للموقنين و في انفسكم افلا تبصرون﴾ (الذاريات/ 21-20)

"In the earth are signs for those having sure faith; and in yourselves; what, do you not see?"

(Sūrah 51:20-21)

﴿ان في خلق السموات و الارض و اختلاف الليل والنهار لآيات لاولي الالباب، الذين يذكرون الله قياماً و قعوداً و علي جنوبهم و يتفكرون في خلق السموات و الارض ربنا ما خلقت هذا باطلاً سبحانك فقنا عذاب النار﴾ (آل عمران/ 191-190)

"Surely in the creation of the heavens and the earth and in the alternation of the night and day there are signs for men possessed of minds who remember God, standing and sitting and on their side, and reflect upon the creation of the heavens and the earth: 'O Lord, Thou hast not created this out of falsehood. Glory be to Thee! Guard us against the chastisement of the Fire.'"

(Sūrah 3:190-191)

﴿انّ في خلق السموات والارض و اختلاف الليل و النهار و الفلك التي تجري في البحر بما ينفع الناس و ما انزل الله من السماء من ماء فاحيا به الارض بعد موتها و بثّ فيها من كل دابّة و تصريف الرياح و السحاب المسخر بين السماء والارض لآيات لقوم يعقلون﴾ (البقرة/ 164)

"Surely in the creation of the heavens and the earth and the alternation of night and day and the ship that runs in the sea with profit to men, and the water God sends down from heaven therewith reviving the earth after it is dead and His scattering abroad in it all manner of crawling thing, and the turning about of the winds and clouds compelled between heaven and earth–surely there are signs for a people having understanding."

(Sūrah 2:164)

As can be seen from the foregoing verses, God refers to all existing things in the universe as the "signs" of their Creator, and the system of the universe as the imprint of an omniscient designer and programmer. The study of the universe and whatever exists in it is considered as one of the most important means for acquiring the knowledge of God and the recognition of the majesty of its Creator. The prophets also based their invitation on the belief in this point. The Prophet Moses (A) made a similar argument in his confrontation with Pharaoh. The Qur'an quotes Moses as putting his argument in these words:

﴿قال ربناالذي اعطي كل شيئ خلقه ثم هدي ... الذي جعل لكم الارض مهداً و سلك فيها سبلاً و انزل من السماء ماءً فاخرجنا به ازواجاً من نبات شتي﴾ (طه/ 53-50)

"He said, 'Our Lord is He who gave everything its creation, then guided it... He who appointed the earth to be a cradle for you and therein threaded roads for you and sent down water out of heaven, and therewith We have brought forth diverse kinds of plants."

(Sūrah 20:50-53)

Prophet Noah (A) is quoted in the Qur'an as saying to his people:

﴿قال رب اني دعوت قومي ليلاً و نهاراً فلم يزدهم دعائي الّا فراراً ... فقلت استغفروا ربكم انّه كان غفاراً ... الم تروا كيف خلق الله سبع سموات طباقاً و جعل القمر فيهن نوراً و جعل الشمس سراجاً والله انبتكم من الارض نباتاً ثم يعيدكم فيها و يخرجكم اخراجاً والله جعل لكم الارض بساطاً لتسلكوا منها سبلاً فجاجاً﴾ (نوح/ 20-5)

"He said, 'My Lord, I have called my people by night and by day, but my calling has only increased them in flight ... and I said, Ask you forgiveness of your Lord; surely He is ever All-forgiving ... Have you not regarded how God created seven heavens one upon another, and set the moon therein for a light and the sun for a lamp? And God cause you to grow out of the earth, then He shall return you into it, and bring you forth. And God has laid the earth for you as a carpet, and thereof you may tread ways, ravines.'"

(Sūrah 71:5-20)

Obviously, it is not for everyone to be able to read the 'book' of the universe. The Qur'an considers only men of knowledge to be capable of benefiting from the book of nature, as can be seen from the following verse:

﴿الم تران الله انزل من السماء ماءً فاخرجنا به ثمرات مختلفاً الوانها و من الجبال جدد بيض و حمر مختلف الوانها و غرابيب سود و مَن الناس والدواب والانعام مختلف الوانه كذلك انّما يخشيالله من عباده العلماؤا﴾ (فاطر/ 28-27)

"Hast thou not seen how that God sends down out of heaven water, and therewith We bring forth fruits of diverse hues? And in the mountains are streaks White and red, of diverse hues, and pitchy black; men too, and beasts and cattle, – diverse are their

hues. Even so only those of His servants fear God who have knowledge; surely God is Almighty, All-forgiving."

(Sūrah 35:27-28)

The Qur'an regards only men of knowledge as being capable of discerning the majesty and magnificence of God's creation and as possessing the humility produced by their knowledge of Divine power and greatness. This point is stressed in some other verses of the Qur'an:

﴿و تلك الامثال نضربها للناس و مايعقلها الا العالمون﴾ (العنكبوت/ 43)

"And these similitude's – We strike them for the people, but none understands them save those who know."

(Sūrah 29:43)

﴿بل هو آيات في صدور الذين اوتوا العلم و ما يجحد بآياتنا الا الظالمون﴾
(العنكبوت/ 49)

"Nay; rather it is signs, clear signs in the breasts of those who have been given knowledge; and none denies Our signs but the evildoers."

(Sūrah 29:49)

Obviously, as implied by the abovementioned verses, an understanding of the "signs" of the Creator, is considered possible only for the learned and the men of knowledge who have strived to fathom the secrets of nature and have acquired knowledge in their fields of study. Otherwise, only a superficial acquaintance with the "book of creation" is not very revealing. A suitable initiation into the book of nature can only be achieved through such sciences as mathematics, physics, chemistry, astronomy, botany, zoology (which we shall refer to as 'natural sciences'). It is with the aid of these and the rational sciences that we discover the laws of nature and unravel the wonderful order and scheme of creation that underlies nature. It is in this light that we should read the verses of the Qur'an such as the following:

﴿فارجع البصر هل تري من فطور ثم ارجع البصر كرتين ينقلب اليك البصر خاسئاً و هو حسير﴾ (ملك/ 4-3)

"You see not in the creation of the All-merciful any imperfection. Return your gaze; Do you see any fissure? Then return your gaze, and again your gaze comes back to you dazzled, a weary."

(Sūrah 67:3-4)

It means that the further human knowledge makes progress in understanding God's creation, the more His Greatness and Majesty will become obvious to men. Consider the following verse:

﴿سنريهم آياتنا في الآفاق و في انفسهم حتي يتبين انه الحق ...﴾ (فصلت/ 53)

"We shall show them Our signs in the horizons and in themselves, till it is clear to them that it is the truth."

(Sūrah 41:53)

In the above verse God promises revelation of His signs, in the universe without and the world of spirit within, to mankind in future so as to make them convinced that it (the Qur'an) is indeed absolutely the Truth.

Another reason for the study of the natural phenomenon and the scheme of creation is that the knowledge of the laws of nature and characteristics of things and organisms can be useful for improvement of conditions of human life. This aspect is emphasized by numerous verses of the Qur'an of which we quote a few:

﴿و سخّر لكم الليل و النهار والشمس والقمر والنجوم مسخرات بامره انّ في ذلك لآيات لقوم يعقلون و ما ذرأ لكم في الارض مختلفاً الوانه ان في ذلك لاية لقوم يذكرون و هو الذي سخّر البحر لتأكلوا منه لحماً طريا و

تستخرجوا منه حلية تلبسونها و تري الفلك مواخر فيه ولتبتغوا من فضله و لعلكم تشكرون والقي في الارض رواسي ان تميد بكم و انهاراً و سبلاً لعلكم تهتدون و علامات و بالنجم هم يهتدون﴾ (النحل/ 16-12)

"And He subjected to you the night and day, and the sun and moon; and the stars are subjected by His command. Surely in that are signs for people who understand. And that which He has multiplied for you in the earth of diverse hues. Surely in that is a sign for a people who remember. It is He who subjected to you the sea, that you may eat of it fresh flesh, and bring forth out of it ornaments for you to wear; and thou mayest see the ships cleaving through it; and that you may seek of His bounty, and so haply you will be thankful. And He cast on the earth firm mountains, lest it shake with you, and rivers and ways; so haply you will be guided; and waymarks; and by the stars they are guided."

(Sūrah 16:12-16)

﴿الم تروا انّ الله سخّر لكم ما في السموات وما في الارض واسبغ عليكم نعمه ظاهرة و باطنة و من الناس من يجادل في الله بغير علم و لاهدى و لا كتاب منير﴾ (لقمان/ 20)

"Have you not seen how that God has subjected to you whatsoever is in the heavens and earth, and He has lavished on you His blessings, outward and inward? And among men there is such a one that disputes about God without knowledge or guidance or an illuminating book."

(Sūrah 31:20)

﴿و سخّر لكم ما في السموات و ما في الارض جميعاً منه ان في ذلك لآيات لقوم يتفكرون﴾ (الجاثيه/ 13)

"And He has subjected to you what is in the heavens and what is in the earth, all together, from Him. Surely in that are signs for a people who reflect."

(Sūrah 45:13)

﴿والذي خلق الازواج كلها و جعل لكم من الفلك والانعام ما تركبون لتستوا علي ظهوره ثم تذكروا نعمة ربكم اذا استويتم عليه و تقولوا سبحان الذي سخّرلها هذا و ماكنّا له مقرنين﴾ (الزخرف/ 13-12)

"He who created the pairs, all of them, and appointed for you ships and cattle such as you ride, that you be seated on their backs and then remember your Lord's blessing when you are seated on them, and say, 'Glory be to Him, who has subjected this to us, and we ourselves were not equal to it.'"

(Sūrah 43:12-13)

According to the Qur'an, the study of the book of nature reveals to man its secrets and manifests its underlying coherence, consistency and order. It allows men to use the agency of knowledge to uncover the riches and resources hidden in nature and to achieve material welfare through his scientific discoveries. God has appointed man His vicegerent or deputy upon the earth and provided him with unlimited opportunities. It is for him to recognize his own possibilities and benefit from his opportunities and acquire the power and wisdom befitting his role as a 'deputy' of God and a 'sign' of His wisdom and omnipotence:

﴿و هوالذي جعلكم خلائف الارض و رفع بعضكم فوق بعض درجات ليبلوكم فيما آتاكم انّ ربك سريع العقاب و انّه لغفور رحيم﴾ (الانعام/ 165)

"It is He who has appointed you viceroys in the earth, and has raised some of you in ranks above others, that He may try you in

what He has given you. Indeed your Lord is quite in retribution, and He is Forgiving and. Merciful."

(Sūrah 6:165)

In fact, this station of being God's viceroy or deputy upon the earth has been bestowed upon man as a result of his capacity for acquisition of knowledge as borne out by this verse:

﴿و علم آدم الاسماء كلها ثم عرضهم علي الملائكة فقال انبئوني بالسماء هولاء ان كنتم صادقين﴾ (البقرة/ 31)

"He taught Adam all the names then presented them to the angels; then He said: 'Tell me the names of those if you are right.'"

(Sūrah 2:31)

Unfortunately Muslims have since long tended to overlook such verses of the Qur'an as quoted above, while this matter was appreciated by non-Muslims who afterwards monopolized the scientific tradition.

Criterion for the Usefulness of Any Science

So far we have tried to show that the recommendations of the Qur'an and *Sunnah* concerning the acquisition of knowledge is not restricted to the particular teaching of *Shari'ah*, but it equally applies to any knowledge useful for mankind. Now we are going to set the criteria as to what sort of knowledge is useful. To do so, we have to find out and define what the obligation and goal of a Muslim in his earthly life is, the Qur'an says that all return to the Creator.

﴿الا الي الله تصير الامور﴾ (شوري/ 53)

"... To Allah do all affairs eventually come."

(Sūrah 42: 53)

And the purpose of the creation of the jinn and human beings is that worship and seek proximity to the Almighty:

﴿و ما خلقت الجن و الانس الا ليعبدون﴾ (الذاريات/ 56)

"And I have created the jinn and the men except that they should worship Me."

(Sūrah 51: 56)

﴿و ان اعبدوني هذا صراط مستقيم﴾ (يس/ 61)

"And that you should worship Me; this is the right way."

(Sūrah 36: 61)

﴿و ما امروا الا ليعبدوا الله مخلصين له الدين ...﴾ (بينه/ 5)

"And they were not enjoined anything except that they worship Allah, being sincere to Him in obedience."

(Sūrah 98: 5)

Therefore, the main objective of man should be seeking proximity to God and attaining His consent, and focusing his activities in this direction. Anything that brings about this proximity or guides him in that direction is praiseworthy. Thus knowledge is useful only if it is an instrument for obtaining knowledge of God, and His pleasure and proximity; otherwise knowledge itself is an inscrutable veil (*hijāb-eakbar*), whether it is linked with the sciences of nature or the sciences of the *Sharī'ah*. As the Persian poet Sa'di has put it:

جز یاد دوست هرچه کنی عمر ضایع است

جز سرّ عشق هرچه بگوئی بطالت است

سعدی بشوی لوح دل از نقش غیر او

علمی که ره بحق ننماید جهالت است

Life is vain except when recalling Him,

No words are good but (uttering) the secrets of love,

Sa'di! Wash of your heart of all but Him,

The knowledge not leading to Him is ignorance.

It is obvious that worshipping God is not only through prayers, fasting and so on. In fact, any move in the direction of proximity to God is considered as worship. One of the means to help man in his way towards God id knowledge, and of course a knowledge with this characteristics can only be considered valuable. By means of knowledge a Muslim can gain proximity to God in various ways and manners.

First of all, he can increase his cognition of God. Our great Prophet Muhammad ﷺ is related as having said:

﴿ان الله يطاع بالعلم و يعبد بالعلم و خير الدنيا و الآخره مع العلم و شرّ الدنيا و الآخره مع الجهل﴾

"God can be worshipped and served by means of knowledge; bliss in this world and Hereafter comes through knowledge; and adversity of this world and Hereafter lies in ignorance." [24]

Secondly, he can effectively help in the advancement of "Islamic society and realization of Islamic goals":

﴿كلمة الله هي العليا﴾ (توبه/ 40)

"And the word of Allah is the highest."

(Sūrah 9: 40)

A tradition has been quoted from our great Prophet ﷺ:

﴿من جاءه الموت و هو يطلب العلم ليحيي به الاسلام كان بينه و بين الانبياء درجة واحدة في الجنة﴾

"Should death occur to a man who is learning knowledge with the purpose of reviving Islam, his position in paradise will be (only) one stage below (that of) the prophets."[25]

Thirdly, he can guide other people. It is reported from our dear Prophet ﷺ as having said:

﴿قال (ص): رحم الله خلفائي، فقيل و من خلفاؤك؟ قال: الذين يحيون سنّتي و يعلمونها عبادالله﴾

"God will patronize my successors. He was asked, 'Who are your successors?' He answered, those who revive my traditions, and teach them to God's worshipers."[26]

The knowledge employed in the above mentioned ways is deemed to be useful; otherwise, it would not have any real value:

﴿ذلك بان الله هو الحق و انّ ما يدعون من دونه الباطل ...﴾ (لقمان/ 30)

"This is because Allah is the truth, and that which they call upon besides Him is the falsehood ..."

(Sūrah 31: 30)

Our great Prophet ﷺ is related as having said:

﴿من تعلم علماً لغيرالله و اراد به غيرالله فليتبوأ مقعده من النار﴾

"He who learns knowledge for other than God, and his aim be other than God, will abide in fire (hell)."[27]

﴿من ازداد علماً و لم يزدد هديً لم يزدد من الله الّا بعدا﴾

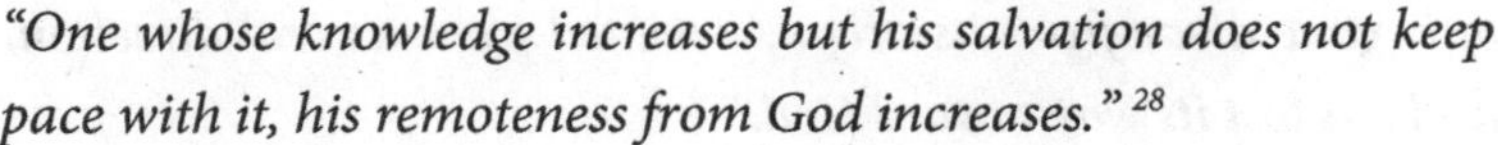

"One whose knowledge increases but his salvation does not keep pace with it, his remoteness from God increases." [28]

﴿ان الله عزوجل يقول تذاكر العلم بين عبادي مما تحيىٰ عليه القلوب الميتة اذا هم انتهوا فيه الي امري﴾

"God, the Most exalted, has said: 'Knowledge discussions among my worshipers can enliven their hearts if it leads them towards my commands'." [29]

Any knowledge not helping man on his way to Allah is similar to the load of books carried on the back of a donkey:

﴿مثل الذين حمّلو التوراة ثم لم يحملوها كمثل الحمار يحمل اسفاراً﴾ (جمعه/5)

"The likeness of those who were charged with the Tawrah, then they did not observe it, is as the likeness of the ass bearing books ..."

(Sūrah 62: 5)

Sayyid Qutb in his commentary on the verse (16: 35) makes the following comment:

"In this verse the subject matter of the knowledge has not been mentioned, for it considers knowledge in general. Moreover, it implies that all kinds of knowledge are considered the gift of God, and any learned man should realize the origin of his knowledge and turn his face towards God to thank Him. He should also utilize it in attaining the consent of God, who has granted him that knowledge. Therefore, knowledge should not stand between man and his creator, for knowledge which causes separation between man's heart and God is nothing but aberration and had gone astray from its origin and is oblivious of the destination. It brings happiness neither to its possessor not to others, and has

only gone away from its origin, deviated from its real direction, and has lost its way toward God." [30]

Hence we can draw the following conclusions:

a) All sciences, whether theological or natural are means for obtaining proximity to God, and as long as they play this role, they are sacred. But this sanctity is not intrinsic.

b) In this perspective, various sciences are not alien to each other because in their own way they interpret the various pages of the book of creation to us. As the eminent poet-sage Shaikh Mahmūd Shabistarī says:

بنـزد آنکـه جانش در تجلـی است

همـه عالـم کتاب حق تعالـی است

از او هر عالمی چون سوره‌ای خاص

یکی زان فاتحه و آن دیگر اخـلاص

"To him whose spirit is enlightened,

The entire universe is a sacred book of the Most High;

Every sphere of universe is a different chapter,

One is the Opening Surah, and another the Surah of Unity."

In this pages of this Divine book, some chapters may have precedence any priority over others, but all of them are essential for the appreciation of God's signs in *'āfāq* (horizons) and *anfus* (souls), that is in the universe without and the universe within.

Decline of Sciences in the Islamic World

In the early centuries of Islamic civilization, when it was at its peak, the Muslim intellectuals approached the question of learning with a vision similar to the one discussed above. Different sciences were seen in a single perspective and considered as branches of the 'tree' of knowledge. The goal of all sciences was seen as the discovery of unity and coherence in the world of nature. Accordingly, the source of all knowledge was considered as being one. They utilized the experimental as well as the intellectual and intuitive approaches for the understanding of various levels and stages of existence. During that period we find numerous examples of scholars who combined authority in religious sciences with encyclopedic knowledge of the natural sciences. Men like Ibn Sina, 'Umar Khayyam, Khwajah Nasir al-Din Tusi and Qutb al-Din Shirazi are eminent examples. As long as this vision and perspective ruled over Muslim scholarship and science, the Muslims were at the vanguard of the human civilization and their cities were centers of specialized learning.

George Sarton admits that during the period between A.D. 750 and 1100, Muslims were undisputed leaders of the intellectual world and between A.D. 1100 and 1350 the centers of learning in the Muslim world retained their global importance and attraction.[31] After 1350 the European world began to advance and the Islamic world not only became stagnant but also failed to absorb the progress made elsewhere. The theological schools excluded all natural sciences from their curriculum, except astronomy and mathematics: This restriction imposed on the religious schools (*madrasah*'s) led to grave repercussions for the Islamic world. Here we point out a few of these effects:

1. Whereas the Europeans were striving to unravel the hidden laws of nature and to discover ways of exploiting its treasures and resources, the Muslims set aside these activities, and left to others what they deserved most to handle. Today, they have reached the

point where they have to depend on America and Europe to satisfy their elementary needs. They remain largely unable to use their resources, and they continue to leave to foreigners to exploit them.

2. Those Muslims who pursued the experimental sciences were mostly estranged from the religious sciences. Accordingly, they lacked the Islamic world-view which was replaced by the atheistic vision that still dominates the Western scientific tradition.
3. The elimination of the study of the natural sciences from the curricula of the religious schools and the lack of direct contact with the sources of modern science, on the part of religious scholars, gave rise to two deviated intellectual currents in the Muslim world:
    a) Some Muslims, under the influence of Western scientific and technical progress and without any knowledge of the limitations of empirical sciences, became singularly possessed with them. To the extent that they even tried to interpret the Qur'an and *hadith* according to their findings. The Qur'anic exegeses written by Tantawi and Sir Sayyid Ahmad Khan belong to this class. Others have gone still further, claiming that all the findings of the modern sciences are found in the Qur'an and the texts of Islamic tradition *(hadith)*. The claim, supposedly, was aimed at demonstrating the miraculous and Divine nature of the Qur'an.[32]

       In the introduction to his exegesis of the Qur'an, Shaikh Mahmud Shaltut, the late head of Al-Azhar University, writes:

"God did not send down the Qur'an to inform mankind of scientific theories and technological techniques ... If we try to

attempt a conciliation between Qur'an and indurable scientific hypotheses, we will thereby subject it to reversals of times to which all scientific theories and hypotheses are prone. That would result in presenting the Qur'an in an apologetic and defensive perspective. Whatever is mentioned in the Qur'an about the mysteries of creation and natural phenomena is intended to impel mankind to speculation and inquiry into these matters so that thereby their faith in it is enhanced." [33]

b) Some scholars of religion have considered scientific theories as opposed to the doctrines of religion and accordingly set out to attack science. This has caused many Muslims to turn away from religion. Had the natural sciences not been exiled from the religious curricula, this tragedy would have not occurred. Any fruitful criticism of ideas based on scientific theories requires, in the first place, familiarity with the various experimental disciplines within modern science, so that any unwarranted conclusions derived from scientific findings may be properly exposed and rejected. How is it possible to claim that the natural sciences result in man's estrangement from God, when the Qur'an unambiguously declares:

﴿انّ في خلق السموات والارض و اختلاف الليل و النهار لآيات لاولي الالباب الذين يذكرون الله قياماً و قعوداً و علي جنوبهم و يتفكرون في خلق السموات والارض ربّنا ما خلقت هذا باطلاً سبحانك فقنا عذاب النار﴾ (آل عمران/ 191-190)

"Surely in the creation of the heavens and earth and in the alternation of night and day there are signs for men possessed of minds who remember God, standing and sitting and on their sides, and reflect upon the creation of the heavens and the earth:

'Our Lord, Thou hast not created this for vanity. Glory be to Thee! Guard us against the chastisement of the Fire.'"

(Sūrah 3:190-191)

If the line of demarcation between religion and science is made clear, there is no reason for any conflict between these two. In fact they would complement each other. Science is like the lamp of life and religion its guide.

Proposals

We have seen how Islam has strongly emphasized the need for acquisition of knowledge in its widest sense, and how the Muslims, following the teachings of Islam, created a brilliant civilization and were the leaders of human intellectual advancement for centuries. We also saw how the separation of religion from science in Muslim societies caused the Muslims to abandon their role of intellectual leadership of mankind. But now that the Muslim community is showing gradual reawakening, and enthusiasm has emerged in almost every corner of the Muslim world, the time seems most suitable for taking decisive steps towards bringing about a scientific renaissance. In this context, we call the attention of our honoured reader to the following proposals:

1. Like the scholars and scientists of the early centuries of the Islamic civilization, we should acquire the knowledge of all useful sciences from others. We can liberate scientific knowledge from its attending Western materialistic interpretations and rehabilitate it in the context of Islamic world-view.
2. The kind of alliance which existed between religious and natural sciences during the peak days of Islamic civilization should be re-established, since, as has been pointed out, there is no separation between the ends of religion and science. Religion teaches that all

creation is oriented towards God as stated in the Qur'anic verse:

﴿يسبح لله ما في السموات و ما في الارض الملك القدوس العزيز الحكيم﴾
(جمعه/ 1)

"All that is in the heavens and the earth magnifies God, the Supreme, the All holy, the Almighty, the All-wise."

(Sūrah 62:1)

Modern science is engaged in an attempt to unravel a comprehensive unity in the laws of nature. The present day physicists are involved in an effort of reducing all apparently independent forces of nature to a single fundamental principle and have obtained some success in this field. [34]

For the achievement of this goal, it seems inevitable that the latest scientific findings should be taught in theological centers, and, in the same way, religious sciences should be taught in universities on a comparatively advanced level. This will be instrumental in familiarizing Muslim research scholars with the Islamic world-view. Moreover, it would give the opportunity to theological schools to utilise latest scientific findings for the interpretation and elucidation of the laws of the *Shari 'ah.*

3. For the achievement of a comprehensive independence of the Islamic *ummah*, it is essential that all the Muslim countries take steps towards the training of specialists in all important scientific and industrial fields. Moreover, research centers should be established in all Muslim communities where the Muslim researchers can work without any anxieties or problems, and with all necessary facilities for research, so that they are not forced to take refuge in atheistic environments, and as a result compelled to put their expertise in the service of others.

4. Scientific research should be thought of as a fundamentally

essential and not an ancillary pursuit. The Muslims should think of it as an obligation imposed upon them by the Qur'an so that they do not come to rely and be dependent on others.

Presently, the practice in most Muslim countries is to import the craft of assembly from Eastern and Western countries instead of making a serious attempt in fundamental scientific research. The present trend will never lead Muslim countries to scientific and technological self-sufficiency. Imported technology should be accompanied by indigenous research work.

5. There should be cooperation between Muslim countries in the scientific and technological research. For this purpose, establishment of communication links between their universities can serve as a preliminary ground. Moreover, joint research and development bodies (such as the Geneva-based CERN organization) should be formed by the Muslim countries where Muslim scientists and research scholars can come together. There should be no nationalistic bias in this regard. Such centers were widely prevalent during the past ages of Islamic civilization.

All that has been done hitherto in this connection has been more or less, of a preliminary nature. Now it is time for a decisive step in this direction.

II

The Significance of Physical and Biological Sciences in Islamic Perspective

Introduction

In the Holy Qur'an the word *al-'ilm*, knowledge, and its derivatives are used more than 750 times. The first few verses that were revealed to the Prophet Muhammad ﷺ mention the importance of reading, pen, and teaching for human beings:

> ﴿ اقرأ باسم ربك الذي خلق خلق الانسان من علق اقرأ و ربك الاكرم الذي علم بالقلم علم الانسان ما لم يعلم ﴾ (العلق/ 1-5)
>
> *"Read: in the name of your Lord who created. He created man from something which clings. Read and your Lord is the most generous. Who taught with pen. Taught man what he knew not..."*
>
> (Sūrah 96: 1-5)

And about the creation of Adam, the Qur'an says that even the angels bowed before Adam after he was taught the names:

> ﴿ و علم آدم الاسماء كلها ثم عرضهم علي الملائكة فقال انبئوني باسماء هؤلاء ان كنتم صادقين قالوا سبحانك لاعلم لنا الا ما علمتنا انك انت العليم الحكيم ﴾ (البقرة/ 32-31)

"And He taught Adam the names, all of them; then He presented them unto the angels and said: Now tell Me the names of these if you speak truly. They said 'Glory be to You. We know not save what You hast taught us. Surely You are the All-knowing, the All-Wise'!"

(Sūrah 2: 31-32)

The Qur'an says that those who know are not comparable to those who do not know:

﴿... قل هل يستوي الذي يعلمون و الذين لا يعلمون ...﴾ (الزمر/ 9)

"Say: Are those who know and those who do not know alike?"

(Sūrah 39: 9)

And that only the learned understand:

﴿و تلك المثال نضربها للناس و ما يعقلها الا العالمون﴾ (العنكبوت/ 43)

"And these examples We set fort for the people, but none understands them save those who know."

(Sūrah 29: 43)

And that only those who have knowledge stand in awe of God:

﴿... انما يخشي الله من عباده العلماء ...﴾ (الفاطر/ 28)

"... of all His servants, only those endowed with knowledge stand in awe of God."

(Sūrah 35: 28)

In the Islamic tradition too, there are many words of praise for knowledge and the learned. A number of traditions are attributed to the prophet Muhammad ﷺ in this regard, some of which are quoted below:

﴿طلب العلم فريضة علي كل مسلم﴾

"It is an obligation for every Muslim to seek knowledge." [35]

﴿اطلبوا العلم ولو بالصين﴾

"Seek knowledge even if it be in China." [36]

﴿اطلبوا العلم من المهد الي اللحد﴾

"Seek knowledge from cradle to grave." [37]

﴿العلماء ورثة الانبياء﴾

"Scholars are the heirs of the prophets." [38]

﴿يوزن يوم القيامة مداد العلماء و دم الشهداء فيرجح مداد العلماء علي دم الشهداء﴾

"The ink of the learned will be weighed with the blood of the martyrs on the Resurrection Day; and, then, the ink of the learned would be preferred to the blood of the martyrs." [39]

It has been a subject of fundamental importance from the early days of Islam as to which kind of knowledge Islam recommends; is there any specific kind of knowledge to be sought? Some well-known Muslim scholars have counted as praiseworthy only those branches of knowledge which are directly connected with religion. As for other types of knowledge they hold the view that it is up to the community to decide which of them are essential for the sustenance of knowledge, and, if there were any limitations of this kind, our Holy Prophet ﷺ would have mentioned them. Furthermore, on the basis of the Qur'an and the Islamic tradition, one can hold that the recommended type of knowledge itself embraces a wide range of subjects.

According to a tradition, Imam Ja'far al-Sādiq (AS), while

addressing himself to Mufaddal ibn ‘Umar, clearly described the vast domain of Islamic Science:

﴿فكر يا مفضل، فيما اعطي الانسان علمه و ما منع، فانه أعطي علم جميع ما فيه صلاح دينه و دنياه. فمما فيه صلاح دينه معرفة الخالق تبارك و تعالي بالدلائل و الشواهد القائمة في الخلق، و معرفة الواجب عليه من‌العدل علي الناس كافة، و برّ الوالدين، و أداء الامانة، و مؤاساة أهل الخلة، و أشباه ذلك مما قد توجد معرفته و الاقرار و الاعتراف به في الطبع و الفطرة، من كل أمة موافقة او مخالفة. و كذلك أعطي علم مافيه صلاح دنياه كالزراعه، و الغراس، و استخراج الارضين، و اقتناء الاغنام، والانعام، و استنباط المياه، و معرفة العقاقير التي يستشفي بها من ضروب الاسقام، و المعادن التي يستخرج منها أنواع الجواهر، و ركوب السفن و الغوص في البحر، و ضروب الحيل في صيد الوحش و الطير و الحيتان، و التصرف في الصناعات، و وجود المتاجر و المكاسب و غير ذلك مما يطول شرحه و يكثر تعداده، مما فيه صلاح أمره في هذه الدار، فأعطي علم ما يصلح به دينه و دنياه، و منع ما سوي ذلك مما ليس في شأنه و لا طاقته أن يعلم، كعلم الغيب و ما هو كائن و بعض ما قد كان ... فانظر كيف أعطي الانسان علم جميع ما يحتاج اليه لدينه و دنياه، و حجب عنه ما سوي ذلك، ليعرف قدره و نقصه. و كلا الامرين فيهما صلاحه ...﴾

“O, Mofaddal! Remember what God has granted man to learn, and what He has forbidden him from knowing. Man may acquire the knowledge of what is good for his life in this world and his faith. In the sphere of religious interests of man are: knowledge of the God, Almighty, through signs and strong proofs that are manifest in the creation; obligatory knowledge of the issues which lead to just treatment of fellowmen; to parents, trustworthiness, helping the poor, and the awareness of the values and principles that every human being, whether believing in God or unbelieving Him, intrinsically and naturally cherishes. Man has also been granted capacity of knowing what is good for his worldly interests. Such knowledge includes the following: agriculture, plantation, cultivation of land, animal husbandry, utilization of pharmaceutically useful plants, exploitation of

mineral resources, navigation and diving the seas, management of various industries, a variety of trades and professions, and many other disciplines profitable to man in this world. Therefore, God has made man capable of attaining all knowledge that he needs for the benefit of his worldly life and faith and He has forbidden what is unfit and beyond his reach such as: occultation, prevision, knowledge of certain past events ... So, look and reflect on how God granted man some capabilities to get what he needs for this world and his religion, while He has deprived him of other abilities so that he may appreciate what he has, and be aware of what he lacks, both of which are to his benefit." [40]

The only limit set to acquisition of knowledge in Islam is that Muslims should seek useful knowledge. Our great Prophet ﷺ is reported as having said:

Any knowledge helping man in performing his God-assigned role in this world is useful, other than that is considered useless knowledge. The following statement which has been reported from Imam al-Sādiq (AS), may be used as a criterion to distinguish between useful and useless kinds of knowledge:

﴿فكلّ ما يتعلم العباد او يعلمون غيرهم من صنوف الصناعات مثل الكتابة و الحساب و التجارة و الصياغة و السراجة و البناء و الحياكة و القصارة و الخياطة و صنعة صنوف التصاوير - ما لم يكن مثل الروحاني - و انواع صنوف الالات التي يحتاج اليها العباد التي منها منافعهم و بها قوامهم و فيها بلغة جميع حوائجهم فحلال فعله و تعليمه و العمل به و فيه لنفسه او لغيره و ان كانت تلك الصناعة و تلك الالة قد يستعان بها علي وجوه الفساد و وجوه المعاصي و يكون معونة علي الحث و الباطل. فلا بأس بصناعته و تعليمه، نظير الكتابة التي هي علي وجه من وجوه الفساد من تقوية معونة ولاة الجور. و كذلك السكين و السيف و الرمح و القوس و غير ذلك من وجوه الآلة التي قد تصرف الي جهات الصلاح و جهات الفساد و تكون الة و معونة عليهما، فلا بأس بتعليمه و تعلمه و اخذ الاجر عليه و فيه و العمل به و فيه لمن كان له فيه جهات الصلاح من جميع الخلائق و محرم عليهم فيه

تصريفه الي جهات الفساد و المضار، فليس علي العالم و المتعلم اثم ولا وزر لما فيه من الرجحان في منافع جهات صلاحهم و قوامهم و بقائهم به و انما الاثم والوزر علي المتصرف بها في وجوه الفساد والحرام. و ذلك انما حرّم الله الفساد التي حرام هي كلها التي يجيء منها الفساد محضا نظير البرابط والمزامير و الشطرنج و كل ملهوبة والصلبان والاقسام و ما اشبه ذلب من صناعات الاشربة الحرام و ما يكون منه و فيه الفساد محضا و لا يكون فيه و لا منه شيء من وجوه الصلاح فحرام تعليمه و تعلّمه و العمل به و اخذ الاجر عليه و جميع التقلب فيه من جميع وجوه الحركات كلها. الا ان تكون صناعة قد تتصرف الي جهات الصنائع، و ان كان قد يتصرف بها و يتناول بها وجه من وجوه المعاصي. فلعله لما فيه من الصلاح حلّ تعلمه و العمل به، و يحرم علي من صرفه الي غير وجه الحق والصلاح ﴾.

"Any sort of science and technology which eliminates man's needs or is useful to God's servants and helps them to continue their lives and meet their daily needs, is permitted by religion to teach or to learn. For example they are: writing, accounting, commerce, work of a goldsmith, saddle-making, brick-laying, knitting, tailoring, painting and drawing (with the exception of animate beings) and making tools required by people. But if such knowledge or skill could be used for vicious and sinful purposes as well as rightful and noble deeds, such as writing which may be abused for strengthening oppressive rulers, is not forbidden; so is making knives, swords, spears, bows and arrows which can be used in both good and bad ways. Teaching and learning such trades or receiving fees for their instruction, provided that it is for the benefit of God's servants, is permissible; but their use in harmful or vicious ways is forbidden; in either case it is not a sin for man to teach or learn such a trade, for utility of these tools is greater than the harm caused by their abuse, and the continuity of social life depends on them. Their misuse, however, is a sinful deed. This is because God has forbidden us to go after anything which is totally corrupt and has no useful result. Thus, it is forbidden to make strings (of musical instruments) flutes, chess,

various instruments of entertainment and pleasure, crosses, idols or the like, and intoxicating drinks, and anything causing disturbance or harm, or ending in corruption and having no use for man, is forbidden to teach, to learn or impart it to others and to obtain fees or wages for them. If there is a crafts, even if it is sometimes used for sinful purposes, it would be permissible to be developed, but using it in the wrong way would be unlawful." [41]

Islam and Science

In this section, we intend to deal with the reasons that justify the study of the sciences (of nature) from the Islamic view-point and then we shall try to see how far the Islamic conception of knowledge is compatible with sciences of nature. The study of the Qur'an and the Islamic tradition indicates that for two fundamental reasons Islam recognized the significance of science:

1. The role of science in knowing God.
2. The role of science in the stability and advancement of the Islamic society.

1. The Role of Science in Knowing God

In the Holy Qur'an there are mote than 750 verses which refer to natural phenomena, and people are asked to think over them in order to recognize Allah through His signs. These verses can be divided into the following categories:

1. The verses that either describe the constituent elements of objects or enjoin man to discover them. For example we read in the Qur'an:

﴿فلينظر الإنسان ممّ خلق﴾. (الطارق/5)

"So let man consider of what he is created."

(Sūrah 86: 5)

﴿والله خلق كلّ دابّة من ماء﴾. (النور/ 45)

"And Allah has created every living creature from water."

(Sūrah 24: 45)

﴿انّا خلقنا الانسان من نطفة امشاج نبتليه فجعلناه سميعا بصيرا﴾ (الانسان/ 2)

"We created man of a sperm-drop, a mingling, trying him; and We made him hearing, seeing."

(Sūrah 76: 2)

2. The verses that either give an account of the manner of creation of material objects or enjoin man to discover their genesis. The following are typical of this category:

﴿و هو الذي خلق السموات والارض في ستّة ايّام و كان عرشه علي الماء ...﴾ (هود/ 7)

"And it is He who created the heavens and the earth in six periods, and His Dominion was upon the waters ..."

(Sūrah 11:7)

﴿و لقد خلقنا الانسان من سلالة من طين ثم جعلناه نطفة في قرار مكين ثم خلقنا النطفة علقة فخلقنا العلقة مضغة فخلقنا المضغة عظاما فكسونا العظام لحما ثم انشأناه خلقا آخر فتبارك الله احسن الخالقين﴾. (المؤمنون/ 12-14)

"And certainly We created man of an extract of clay, then We made him a small life-germ in a firm resting place. Then We

made the life-germ a clot, then We made the clot a tissue, then We made the tissue bones, then We clotted the bones with flesh, then We caused it to grow into another creation, so blessed be Allah, the best of the Creators."

(Sūrah 23: 12-14)

﴿اولم يرالذين كفروا انّ السموات والارض كانتا رتقا ففتقناهما ...﴾ (الانبياء / 30)

"Do not those who disbelieve see that the heavens and the earth were closed up which We then parted asunder ..."

(Sūrah 21: 30)

﴿خلق السموات بغير عمد ترونها والقي في الارض رواسي ان تميد بكم ...﴾ (لقمان/ 10)

"He created the heavens without pillars you can see, and He cast on the earth firm mountains, lest it shakes with you ..."

(Sūrah 31: 10)

﴿ثم استوي الي السماء و هي دخان﴾ (فصلت/ 11)

"Then He directed himself to the heaven when it was a vapour..."

(Sūrah 41: 11)

﴿افلا ينظرون الي الابل كيف خلقت و الي السماء كيف رفعت و الي الجبال كيف نصبت و الي الارض كيف سطحت.﴾ (الغاشيه/ 17-20)

"Will they not then consider how the camel was created, how heaven was lifted up, how the mountains were hoisted, how the earth was outstretched."

(Sūrah 88: 17-20)

3. The verses in which man is enjoined to discover how our physical universe came into existence. The following are typical of this kind of verses:

﴿قل سيروا في الارض فانظروا كيف بدأالخلق ...﴾ (العنكبوت/ 20)

"Say: journey in the earth, then behold how He originated creation ..."

(Sūrah 29: 20)

﴿أولم يروا كيف يبديء الله الخلق ثم يعيده﴾ (العنكبوت/ 19)

"Have they not seen how God originated creation, then brings it back again..."

(Sūrah 29: 19)

4. The verses in which man is enjoined to study natural phenomena. The following verses typify this category:

﴿الم تر انّ الله انزل من السماء ماء فسلكه ينابيع في الارض ثم يخرج به زرعا مختلفا الوانه، ثم يهيج فترٰيه مصفرا ثم يجعله حطاما ان في ذلك لذكري لاولي الالباب﴾ (الزمر/ 21)

"Do you not see that Allah sends down water from the heaven (cloud), then makes it go along in the earth in springs, then brings forth there with herbage of various colours, then it withers so that you see it becoming yellow, then He makes it a thing crushed and broken into pieces? Most surely there is a reminder for the men of understanding."

(Sūrah 39: 21)

﴿ان في خلق السموات و الارض و اختلاف الليل و النهار والفلك التي

تجري في البحر بما ينفع الناس و ما انزل الله من السماء من ماء فاحيا به الارض بعد موتها و بثّ فيها من كل دابّة و تصريف الرياح و السحاب المسخّر بين السماء والارض لآيات لقوم يعقلون﴾ (البقرة/ 164)

"Surely in the creation of heavens and the earth and the alternation of night and day and the ship that runs in the sea with profit to men, and the water God descends down from heaven therewith reviving the earth after it is dead and his scattering abroad in it all manner of crawling things and the turning about of the winds and the clouds compelled between heaven and earth, there are signs for a people having understanding."

(Sūrah 2: 164)

5. The verses in which God swears by various natural objects. Here we cite some examples:

﴿والشمس وضحيها والقمر اذا تليها والنهار اذا جلّيها والليل اذا يغشيها والسماء و ما بنيها والارض و ما طحيها ...﴾ (الشمس/ 1-6)

"By the sun and his morning brightness, and by the moon when she follows him, and by the day when it displays him and by the night when it enshrouds him and by the heaven and that which built it and by the earth and that which extended it ..."

(Sūrah 91: 1-6)

﴿فلا اقسم بمواقع النجوم و أنه لقسم لو تعلمون عظيم﴾ (الواقعه/ 76-75)

"But nay! I swear by the fallings of stars. And most surely it is a very great oath if you only know."

(Sūrah 56: 75-76)

6. The verses in which by reference to some natural phenomena the possibility of the occurrence of Resurrection has been explained.

Examples:

﴿يا ايّهاالناس ان كنتم في ريب من البعث فانّا خلقناكم من تراب ثم من نطفة من علقة ثم من مضغة مخلقة و غير مخلّقة ... و تري الارض هامدة، فاذا انزلنا عليها الماء اهتزت و ربت و انبتت من كل زوج بهيج﴾ (الحج/ 5)

"O people! If you are in doubt about the raising, then surely we created you from dust, then from a small life-germ, then from a clot, then from a lump of flesh, complete in make and incomplete ... and you see the earth's sterile land but when We send down on it the water, it stirs and swells and brings forth of every kind a beautiful garbage."

(Sūrah 22: 5)

﴿اوليس الذي خلق السموات و الارض بقادر علي ان يخلق مثلهم بلي و هو الخلّاق العليم﴾ (يس/ 81)

"Is not He who created the heavens and the earth able to create the like of them? Yes! And He is the Creator (of all), the Knower."

(Sūrah 36: 81)

﴿يخرج الحيّ من الميّت و يخرج الميّت من الحيّ و يحيي الارض بعد موتها و كذلك تخرجون﴾ (الروم/ 19)

"He brings forth the living from the dead and brings forth dead from the living, and gives life to the earth after its death, and thus shall you be brought forth."

(Sūrah 30: 19)

7. The verses that emphasize the thoroughness and orderliness of the creations of Allah. The following verses envisage this point:

﴿و تري الجبال تحسبها جامدة و هي تمر مرّالسحاب، صنع الله الذي اتقن كل شيء ...﴾ (النمل/ 88)

"And you shall see the mountains, that you supposed fixed, passing by like clouds, God's handiwork, who has created everything very well ..."

(Sūrah 27: 88)

﴿الذي خلق سبع سموات طباقا، ما تري في خلق الرحمن من تفاوت، فارجع البصر هل تري من فطور ثم ارجع البصر كرتين، ينقلب اليك البصر خاسئا و هو حسير﴾ (الملك/ 4-3)

"Who created seven heavens one upon another. You see no imperfection in the creation of the Beneficent God; then look again, can you see any disorder? Then return back the eye again and again, your look shall come back to you dazzled, a weary."

(Sūrah 67: 3-4)

﴿والارض مددناها والقينا فيها رواسي وانبتنا فيها من كل شيء موزون﴾ (الحجر/ 19)

"And the earth, We stretched it forth, and cast on it firm mountains, and We caused to grow in it of everything justly weighed."

(Sūrah 15: 19)

﴿و خلق كل شيء فقدره تقديرا﴾ (الفرقان/ 2)

"And He created everything, then, He ordained it very exactly.

(Sūrah 25: 2)

﴿خلق السموات والارض بالحق يكوّر الليل علي النهار و يكوّر النهار علي

الليل و سخّر الشمس والقمر كل يجري لاجل مسمّي ...﴾ (الزمر/ 5)

"He created the heavens and the earth in truth, wrapping night about the day, and wrapping day about the night, and He has subjected the sun and the moon, each of them running to an assigned term."

(Sūrah 39: 5)

﴿و ما خلقنا السماء والارض و ما بينهما لاعبين﴾ (الأنبياء / 16)

"And We did not create the heaven and the earth and what is between them sport."

(Sūrah 21: 16)

8. The verses that explain the harmony in which man exists with the rest of the physical universe and the subservience of what is in the earth and in the heavens to man. Following exemplify this type of verses:

﴿هو الذي خلق لكم ما في الارض جميعا﴾ (البقرة/ 29)

"It is He who created for you all that is in the earth."

(Sūrah 2: 29)

﴿و سخّر لكم ما في السموات و ما في الارض جميعا منه ...﴾ (الجاثية/ 13)

"And He has made subservient to you what is in the heavens and what is in the earth, all together from him ..."

(Sūrah 45: 13)

﴿هوالذي جعل لكم الارض ذلولا فامشوا في مناكبها و كلوا من رزقه ...﴾ (الملك/ 15)

"It is He Who made the earth submissive to you; therefore walk in its tracts, and eat of His provisions ..."

(Sūrah 67: 15)

﴿و الانعام خلقها لكم فيها دفء و منافع و منها تأكلون﴾ (النحل/ 5)

"And He created the cattle for you; you have in them warm clothing and many advantages, and of them you eat."

(Sūrah 16: 5)

﴿و انزلنا الحديد فيه بأس شديد و منافع للناس﴾ (الحديد/ 25)

"And We sent down iron, wherein is great might, and many uses for men ..."

(Sūrah 57: 25)

﴿و هوالذي جعل لكم النجوم لتهتدوا بها في ظلمات البرّ و البحر، قد فصّلنا الأيات لقوم يعلمون﴾ (الانعام/ 97)

"And He is who has made the stars for you that you might follow the right way thereby by the darkness of the land and sea; truly we have made plain the communications for a people who know."

(Sūrah 6: 97)

In these verses the Almighty invites His servants to see and reflect upon the natural phenomena and, through the observation of order and coordination in the system of creation and its wonders, get closer to His. It is obvious that for having a clear conception of the issues referred to in these verses, and for the discovery of the answers to the problems therein one has to be familiar with the natural and physical sciences, because a superficial knowledge of natural phenomena cannot reveal the grandeur of Creation to man. It is for this very reason that in the verses 27-28 of the chapter *Fātir*, after describing a number of natural phenomena, God says:

﴿... انّما يخشي الله من عباده العلماء ...﴾ (فاطر/ 28-27)

"... of His servants only those who are possessed of knowledge fear Allah ..."

(Sūrah 35: 27-28)

﴿بل هو آيات بينات في صدور الذين اوتوا العلم ...﴾ (العنكبوت/ 49)

"Nay, these are clear signs in the breasts of those who have been given knowledge ..."

(Sūrah 29: 49)

On the other hand, the knowledge of natural phenomena is effective in leading us closer to God only if we have faith. The following verse asserts this point beautifully:

﴿قل انظروا ماذا في السموات والارض و ما تغني الايات والنذر عن قوم لا يؤمنون﴾ (يونس/ 101)

"Say: Behold what is in the heavens and in the earth; but neither signs nor warnings avail a people who do not believe."

(Sūrah 10: 101)

One should not forget, however, that the Qur'an is not a handbook of experimental science and if it explains some natural phenomena, it is because of the following reasons:

i) The study of natural phenomena and wonders of creation strengthens man's faith in God.

ii) By becoming familiar with the opportunities that God has provided for man, he becomes more knowledgeable about Allah and by obtaining just benefits from them, he can offer his gratitude to Him.

In fact, it was due to the encouragement of the Qur'an that Muslim scientists became deeply involved in acquiring scientific knowledge. The development of Islamic civilization, too, was to a great extent indebted to the Qur'anic outlook. The prominent Muslim scientists of the past acknowledged their indebtedness to the Qur'an, an indebtness that even some Western scholars have confirmed. For example Levy, in *The Social Structure of Islam*, says:

"Apart from a small number of investigators inspired by Greek philosophic ideals, the Muslims who engaged in the pursuit of science did so ... in order to discover, in the wonders of nature, the signs or tokens of the glory of God." [42]

George Sarton, in his book *Introduction to the History of Science* writes that in order to fully conceive the motive behind the fields of science, one should note the axial role of the Qur'an for them. [43]

In his book, the *Kitāb al-Tahdīd Nihāyāt al-'Amākin*, Al-Biruni writes:

"When a person decides to discriminate between truth and falsehood, he has to study the universe and find out whether it is eternal or created. If somebody thinks that he does not need this kind of knowledge, he is however in need of thinking about the laws that govern our world, in part or in its entirety. This leads him to know the truth about them, and paves the way for knowing the being, who directs and controls the universe, and His attributes. This is, in fact, the kind of truth that God enjoined His knowledgeable servants to search for, and Allah spoke the truth when He said:

﴿... و يتفكرون في خلق السموات والارض، ربّنا ما خلقت هذا باطلا ...﴾

(آل عمران/ 191)

"... and reflect upon the creation of the heavens and the earth: our Lord You have not created this in vain ..."

(Sūrah 3: 191)

"This verse contains what I explained in detail, and if man works according to it, he can have access to all branches of knowledge and cognition." [44]

Also in Al-Biruni's *Kitāb al-Jamāhir* we read:

"Sight connects what we see to the signs of Divine wisdom in creation and deduces the existence of the Creator." [45]

In that part of his diary which belongs to the year 417 *Hijrah*, Ibn al-Haytham writes:

"From my very childhood I have been wondering about various peoples (i.e. sects) and their beliefs. Each sect has its own opinions and beliefs according to the principles of its faith. I, therefore, began to doubt the views of various sects, and I am now convinced that truth is one and the same and their differences are based on the ways and methods of finding the truth. Anyhow, having gained an insight into the intellectual basis, I decided to search for the truth and tear away the veil of superstitions and doubts, which an illusive vision has cast on the people, and so that the doubting and skeptical people may lift their gaze freed from the labyrinth of skepticism. Afterwards, I decided to discover as to what is that brings us closer to God, what pleased him most, and what makes us submissive to his ineluctable Will. My feeling were akin to those of Gallen, which he describes in the seventh chapter of his Hilat-ul-bur. While addressing his pupils, he says:

'I am not aware of the feelings, thoughts, and sensations which have guided me since my childhood. Call it what you may, a matter of chance or intuition, vouchsafed by Almighty God or madness. You may attribute the source of my inspiration to any of the three. I shunned the publications, looked at them with contempt and derision and did not incline toward their company. I constantly sought knowledge and truth, and it became my belief that for gaining access to the effulgence and closeness of God, there is no better way than that of search for truth and knowledge. At last I was led to the conclusion that Truth can only be discovered by the formulations of theories, the content of which is sense and their form is intellectual equipment. I found such theories present in the logic, physics, and theology of Aristotle ...'

When this matter became clear, I decided to understand philosophy, which consisted of mathematics, physics and metaphysics, whole-heartedly ... Therefore, I learnt their principles and in that way I acquired skill in their derivatives ... Realizing the mortality of man, ... I had acquired in these three disciplines, and wrote some books in the explanation of the difficulties in relation to their derivatives. This has been going on till now, i.e. 417 A.H."[46]

We see that Muslim scientists' quest for knowledge of natural phenomena was due to the fact that they considered this course of study to be one of the best ways of approaching God. They believed that by studying signs of God in nature they can discover the interrelation between all parts of the universe and the unity hidden behind this world of multiplicity, and this in turn leads them to the unique Creator.

In the glorious period of Islamic civilization, Muslim scientists assimilated cosmological sciences of their time into their view, were trying to demonstrate the unity of nature, and were searching for the primary Cause of things, and thus were conformed to the Islamic perspective. In this process, however, they first drew out the foreign elements, and then infused the rest with the Islamic concepts. Furthermore, Muslim scientists employed both experimental and theoretical methods of investigation.

Unfortunately, this kind of outlook toward the sciences of nature was gradually discarded in the Islamic world and Muslims neglected the recommendations of the Holy Qur'an about the study of nature and about taking advantage of the opportunities that God has provided for man. On the other hand, non-Muslims studied these subjects, and this gave them mastery over the rest of the world. An important consequence of this grave mistake was that a large gap appeared between religion and the mundane affairs of Muslims and they were forced to try to learn science and technology from the West. A by-product of this has been the infiltration of undesirable features of Western civilization into the Islamic world. As a consequence of these unfortunate facts, Muslims have reached a point where they have lost their spiritual qualities, and are not capable of controlling their mundane affairs without foreign assistance.

❁

2. The Role of Science in the Advancement of an Islamic Society

According to the Holy Qur'an, Islam is a Universal religion:

﴿قل يا ايها الناس إنّي رسول الله اليكم جميعا﴾ (الاعراف/ 158)

"Say: O' mankind surely I am the Messenger of God to you all."

(Sūrah 7: 158)

﴿و ما ارسلناك الّا كافة للناس بشيرا و نذيرا﴾ (سبأ/ 28)

"And We have not sent you but to all mankind as a bearer of good news and as a warner."

(Sūrah 34: 28)

The aim of Islam is to establish a monotheistic society in which God's word is the highest:

﴿و جعل كلمة الذين كفروا السفلي و كلمة الله هي العليا﴾ (التوبة/ 40)

"And He made the word of the unbelievers the lowest, and God's word the uppermost."

(Sūrah 9: 40)

In order to establish such a society and to keep it immune from the dangers of the unbelievers, the Islamic world has to be completely independent. The following verse envisages this point:

﴿و لن يجعل الله للكافرين علي المؤمنين سبيلا﴾ (النساء/ 141)

"And God will not grant the unbelievers any way over the believers."

(Sūrah 4: 141)

Moreover, our Prophet Muhammad ﷺ is reported to have said:

﴿الاسلام يعلوا و لا يعلي عليه﴾

"Islam is superior to (all) others and nothing can surpass it."[47]

Obviously, in order to guarantee the superiority of Islamic society over others, Muslims should try to make themselves independent and self-sufficient. It is for this reason that Muslim jurisprudents have given the verdict that any deed leading to the supremacy of unbelievers over the Muslims is forbidden.[48] Moreover, they have decreed that it is a duty of an Islamic society to provide whatever is needed for the sustenance of the society. In the Holy Qur'an itself Muslims are enjoined to prepare and equip themselves in every respect to face the challenge of the forces of unbelievers:

﴿واعدّوا لهم مااستطعتم من قوة و من رباط الخيل ترهبون به عدو الله و عدوكم ...﴾ (الانفال/ 60)

"And prepare against them whatever force and strings of horses you can to terrify thereby the enemy of God and your enemy ..."

(Sūrah 8: 60)

Today, everything revolves around the axis of science and technology. Therefore, in order to be independent and self-reliant, Islamic policy should provide all scientific and technological capabilities that are essential for its self-sufficiency and glory. This involves training of specialists of high caliber in every important field of science and technology, and equipping them with the best technical facilities. Unfortunately, since Muslims have overlooked the need to equip themselves with scientific and technological knowledge and have given way to others in these fields, they have become more and more dependent for their very necessities of life on non-Muslims. Ibn Ikhwah (Ibn al-'Ukhuwwa), a *Shāfi'ī* jurisprudent of the seventh century after Hijrah, tells us in his book The *Ma'ālim al-Qurba fī Ahkām al-Hisba*:

> *"Medicine is an art both theoretical and practical the acquisition of which is permitted by the law for the reason that thereby health is safeguarded and weaknesses and sicknesses repelled from this noble structure [of the body]. It [the practice of medicine] is one of the duties for which the community is responsible and yet there is no Muslim to fulfill it. Many a town has no physician who is not a dhimmī [A "protected" non-Muslim-Christian. Jew or Zoroastrain] belonging to a people whose evidence about physicians is not accepted [in the courts] where the laws of medicine are concerned. No [Muslim] occupies*

himself with it ... The town is full of legists occupied with granting fatwās and giving replies to legal queries on points which arise. Can there be any reason for the faith's permitting a state of things in which large numbers occupy themselves with one particular duty while another is neglected, except that by medicine there is no access to judgeships and governorships whereby it is possible to claim superiority over rivals and to acquire authority over enemies." [49]

If Ibn Ikhwah was complaining in the seventh century after *Hijra*, that most of the physicians in the Muslim society of his time were Jews or Christians, and Muslims were neglecting this compulsory duty, today, we see that Muslims are unable to use their resources and they let others exploit them. As the famous Pakistani Poet Iqbal states:

دیروز مسلم از شرفِ علم سربلند

امروز پشت مسلم و اسلامیان خم است

"The Muslim of yesterday was proud and esteemed for his knowledge, (but) today the believers' and Muslims' back is bent (before others)".

Here one may ask, "While the Qur'an says that unbelievers will in no way have domination over the believers, why are Muslims now ruled by unbelievers? The answer may be found in the fact that many of today's Muslims are not serious believers, and they overlook their Islamic obligations. They neither have the unity nor do they go after knowledge and other provisions recommended by the Holy Qur'an:

﴿و اعدوا لهم ماستطعتم من قوة و من رباط الخيل ترهبون به عدوالله و عدوكم ...﴾ (الانفال/ 60)

"And prepare against them what force you can and horses tied at the frontier, to frighten thereby the enemy of Allah and your enemy ..."

(Sūrah 8: 60)

Despite all the categorical orders of the Qur'an, let us see, what we have done in the way of preparing ourselves and exulting Islamic Society. While Islam does not allow the dominance of the unbelievers over believers even in a simple matter, like inheritance, [50] why are Muslims so entirely dependent on the products of others?

It will be useful to have a look at the present state of the Islamic world. There are more than 50 Islamic countries with 1/5 of the total population of the world, and covering 1/5 of the continents of the earth. They possess fifty percent of the oil reserves as well as other natural resources of the world. On the other hand, the Islamic nations depend on non-Islamic countries for their food, technology, science and defence requirements. They consume more food that they can produce. Their export consists mainly of raw materials, the prices of which are falling continually; while their imports are predominantly manufactured products, the prices of which are rising day by day.

It is obvious that in this deplorable condition the Islamic countries will continue their dependence on the West until they fully equip themselves in the way of providing their own food and technology, and even this has to be done in the form of a mobilized combat, without which there seems to be little likelihood of the elimination of Western cultural and economic dominance over Islamic countries. Imam Khomeini in his book *Tahrīr al-Wasīlah* says:

"Should the danger of political and economic domination of the enemy increase to the extent that it might bring the Islamic society under its political and economic yoke (causing humiliation and shame to Islam and Muslims and weakening

them), it would be incumbent on all Muslims to defend their cause with the means and tools similar to those of the enemy." [51]

Here, we find it necessary to mention two important points:

a) From the Islamic viewpoint it is faith which guarantees the proper use of knowledge. In the Qur'an, knowledge and faith stand side by side. In the first verse revealed to the Prophet ﷺ Muhammad, reading has been recommended; but reading stands next to the name of the Creator, which means acquiring knowledge should be in God's name, not in the name of satan. Knowledge together with faith leads to righteousness; whereas knowledge in the hand of unbelievers is a means of destruction. Many abuses of knowledge have been made by the unbelieving scientists. A tradition related to our Prophet ﷺ says:

﴿الا انّ شر الشر شرار العلماء و انّ خير الخير خيار العلماء﴾

"Surely, the worst of all evils are wicked scholars and the best of all good things are good scholars." [52]

As the Persian poet Jalāl al-Dīn Rūmī puts it:

بد گهر را علم و فن آموختن

دادن تیغ است دستِ راهزن

تیغ دادن در کف زنگی مست

به که باشد علم ناکس را بدست

علم و مال و منصب و جاه و قران

فتنه آرد در کفِ بد گوهران

پس غزا زین فرض شد بر مؤمنان

تا ستانند از کف مجنون سنان

"To impart knowledge and arts to villains, is like giving a sword in the hands of a robber;

putting a sword in the hand of a drunk, is a lesser evil than arming a villain with knowledge;

wealth, knowledge and position are the cause of corruption in the hands of ignobles;

therefore, it is incumbent on the believers, to snatch spears from the grip of lunatics."

The Holy Qur'an itself considers religious faith to be an essential factor for attaining all-round superiority.

﴿و لا تهنوا و لا تحزنوا و انتم الاعلون ان كنتم مؤمنين﴾ (آل‌عمران/ 139)

"Faint not, neither sorrow; you shall be the upper ones if you are believers."

(Sūrah 3: 139)

﴿و لو انّ اهل القري آمنوا واتقوا لفتحنا عليهم بركات من السماء والارض ...﴾ (الاعراف/ 96)

"Yet had the peoples of the cities believed and been God fearing, We would have showered upon them blessing from heaven and earth ..."

(Sūrah 7: 96)

﴿... و لله العزة ولرسوله و للمؤمنين ...﴾ (المنافقون/ 8)

"...Yet glory belongs unto God, and unto His Messenger and the believers ..."

(Sūrah 63: 8)

It is to be noted that despite the importance given to learning science and technology, they are not considered to be sufficient in themselves; and Muslims should, in addition to raising their standard in the material and scientific fields, have firm belief in the Islamic ideology and follow the religious principles for attaining the desired goals. Sayyid Qutb elaborates this matter in a convincing manner:

"God has made a clear promise and has given a definite order that if real faith penetrates into the souls of the faithful and is exemplified in their life style and their system of government, and if in all their acts and discourses Muslims pay attention only to Allah ..., then Allah will not grant unbelievers any superiority over the believers. In order to guarantee our victory in every place and at all times, we should give priority to our faith and its requirements ... and it is faith itself that demands from us strength and self-sufficiency. It forbids us to rely on our enemies and to seek help from anybody but Allah." [53]

b) Islam encourages Muslims to equip themselves with science and technology in order to guarantee the independence and development of the Islamic society and for the sake of the preservation of spiritual aspects. Even in the Qur'anic verse:

﴿و اعدوا لهم مااستطعتم من قوة و من رباط الخيل ...﴾ (الانفال/ 60)

"And prepare against them what force you can and horses tied at the frontier to frighten thereby the enemy of Allah and your enemies ..."

(Sūrah 8: 60)

Where God invites Muslims to strengthen their defence; it is immediately added that its aim is the weakening (frightening) of the enemies of God and Muslims. Therefore, while strengthening their material powers, Muslims should employ them in the service of spiritual causes and for the realization of Islamic ideals. They should not seek material progress for its own sake. The following glorious verses propound this idea in clear terms:

﴿انا جعلنا ماعلي الارض زينة لها لنبلوهم ايّهم احسن عملا﴾ (الكهف/ 7)

"Surely We have made whatever is on the earth an embellishment for it, so that We may try them (as to) which of them is best in works."

(Sūrah 18: 7)

﴿و هوالذي خلق السموات والارض في ستة ايّام و كان عرشه علي الماء ليبلوكم أيّكم احسن عملا ...﴾ (هود/ 7)

"And He is Who created the heavens and the earth in six periods and His dominion (extends) on the water so that He might manifest you which of you is best in action."

(Sūrah 11: 7)

Conclusion

We noticed that in Islam, everything revolves around the axis of the unity of God, and that the desirability of science and technology is based on the fact that these are tools that add to our knowledge of God and are effective in the establishment of an independent monotheistic society. In our age, that the Islamic countries are under the influence of the unbelievers, Muslims have a great responsibility on their shoulders. Take into consideration a verse we quoted earlier:

"And prepare against them what force you can and horses tied at the frontier, to frighten thereby the enemy of Allah and your enemy ..."

(Sūrah 8: 60)

According to this Qur'anic injunction, Muslims should prepare and equip themselves in every respect, and since, today empirical sciences play a fundamental role in every aspect of the material life, strengthening of this dimension of Islamic policy is a necessity. The Islamic countries, therefore, should establish centers for promoting scientific and technological research and should train experts of high caliber in all useful fields of science and technology. In this attempt, however, they should put the emphasis on fundamental sciences, so that they shall be able to advance original research rather than imitate others.

On the other hand, in order to ensure the success of scientific renaissance in Islamic policy, several important points should be taken into consideration:

1. It is obvious that at the present time, Muslims need to learn science and technology from the countries that are advanced in these fields, and, of course, this is not by itself a blameworthy action. In fact our Prophet Muhammad ﷺ is reported to have said:

﴿اطلبوا العلم ولو بالصين﴾

"Seek knowledge even if it be in China." [54]

﴿الحكمة ضالة المؤمن فحيث وجدها فهواحق بها﴾

"The believer is always searching for wisdom; wherever he may find it, it is his, because he deserves to have it more than anyone else." [55]

﴿خذوا العلم من افواه الرجال﴾

"Acquire knowledge from what people say." [56]

And Imam 'Ali (AS) is reported to have said:

﴿حق علي العاقل ان يضيف الي رأيه رأي العقلاء و ان يضم الي علمه علوم الحكماء﴾

"It is praiseworthy for every wise man to add the opinions of other sages to that of his own, and add the learners' knowledge to his own knowledge." [57]

﴿العلم ضالة المؤمن، فخذوه ولو من ايدي المشركين﴾

"Knowledge is the lost property of a believer; thus, acquire it even if it is in the polytheists' hands." [58]

The Muslim scholars of the past did the same and what we are supposed to do is to receive knowledge from non-believers in a selective manner, i.e. to purge it from the elements alien to Islam and to remodel it in the light of the Islamic world-view. It is under the guidance of these principles that Muslims can acquire knowledge from non-Muslim sources and mould it to suit the Islamic ideals. It is only under these conditions that different levels of knowledge can be coordinated to attain our aim and can take us closer to God.

2. We should revive the scientific spirit of our learned ancestors and their zeal to reshape different branches of knowledge for making use of them for the development of Islamic civilization. They did not see any real contradiction between the so-called religious sciences and the physical sciences, and they considered the aim of both to be the same. In their view both the biological and physical sciences show the harmony between various parts of the universe, and therefore, they lead us to God – something which is the aim of religion too. It was due to this kind of outlook that religious as well as physical sciences were taught together and some of the Muslim scholars were first-rate authorities in both of them. This praiseworthy tradition has to be

revived again, and the curricula of our universities have to include both religious sciences and the latest scientific and technological advances.

It is only in this way that Muslims can be equipped with the latest developments made in scientific fields and at the same time protect their students against atheistic and materialistic teachings of the East and the West, and can bring science and technology under the guidance of Islamic outlook.

3. According to the Holy Qur'an man is the vicegerent of God on earth:

﴿و اذا قال ربك للملائكة اني جاعل في الارض خليفة ...﴾ (البقرة/ 30)

"And when your Lord said to the angels 'I am going to place in the earth a vicegerent'..."

(Sūrah 2: 30)

﴿هو الذي جعلكم خلائف في الارض فمن كفر فعليه كفره ...﴾ (فاطر/ 39)

"It is He Who appointed you vicegerents in the earth; so whoever disbelieves, his unbelief shall be charged against himself..."

(Sūrah 35: 39)

﴿ثمّ جعلناكم خلائف في الارض من بعدهم لينظر كيف تعلمون﴾ (يونس/ 14)

"Then We appointed you vicegerents in the earth after them, so that We may see how you act."

(Sūrah 10: 14)

Now, in order to be able to play this role, God has given man all kinds of gifts and has endowed him with intelligence and has provided a nice harmony between the creation of man and the rest of the universe so that human beings can take care of their needs. Again to quote the Holy Qur'an:

﴿هو الذي خلق لكم ما في الارض جميعا﴾ (البقرة/ 29)

"He it is Who created for you all that is in the earth."

(Sūrah 2: 29)

﴿و لقد مكناكم في الارض و جعلنا لكم فيها معايش ...﴾ (الاعراف/ 10)

"And certainly We have established you in the earth and made in it means of livelihood for you ..."

(Sūrah 7: 10)

It is therefore for Muslims to employ their knowledge and technology for the solemn goals of Islam and higher interests of humanity in order to exemplify the glorious verse:

﴿كنتم خير امة اخرجت للناس تأمرون بالمعروف و تنهون عن المنكر و تؤمنون بالله ...﴾ (آل عمران/ 110)

"You are the best nation ever brought forth to men, bidding to honour, and forbidding dishonour, and believing in God ..."

(Sūrah 3: 110)

Muslims are not permitted to destroy the earth or spread injustice and corruption upon it. Rather, they are asked to dwell in it in a manner desired by God:

﴿... هو أنشأكم من الارض واستعمركم فيها...﴾ (هود/ 61)

"... He brought you forth from the earth and has made you to dwell in it ..."

(Sūrah 11: 61)

They are supposed to reform it and bring order to it. Unfortunately Western science, due to its misconceived philosophical notions, has brought destruction in its wake. Thus, the knowledgeable and powerful scientists of our time fit the description in the following verse of the Holy Qur'an:

﴿و اذا تولي سعي فيالارض ليفسد فيها و يهلك الحرث و النسل والله لا يحب الفساد﴾ (البقرة/ 205)

"And whenever he prevails, he hastens, about the earth, to do corruption there and to destroy the tillage and the stock: and God does not love corruption."

(Sūrah 2: 205)

The story of Adam, in the Qur'an, while illustrating the superiority of man, due to his being vicegerent of God and his knowledge of the "names" (*'asmā'*), warns us of the dangers that face him whenever he violates God's commandments. Man is appointed as the vicegerent of God on earth in order to reform it, to see the signs of God, and to become representative of His power and Wisdom.

4. In the schools and universities of the Islamic countries, sufficient attention should be paid to the problem of moral purification of students and they ought to be instructed in virtuous actions. It is only then that the graduates of schools and universities will be both faithful and knowledgeable, and it is with this kind of scientists that order can be brought to our world and the well-known saying of Imam 'Ali (AS) exemplified:

﴿و بالايمان يعمر العلم.﴾

"Knowledge prospers through faith." [59]

Knowledge without faith does not produce anything better than what Western civilization has produced, and the faithless scientists have no aim but position, power, and wealth. Imam Khomeini has justly said:

"All of these tools that are made for the destruction of mankind and all of the advances that are made in the field of weaponry are the products of university graduates who have not been morally trained and who have not purified their souls." [60]

The Holy Qur'an itself, when talking about the Prophet's message, mentions spiritual training to be compulsory for learning:

﴿كما ارسلنا فيكم رسولا منكم يتلوا عليكم آياتنا و يزكيهم و يعلمكم الكتاب والحكمة ...﴾ (البقرة/ 151)

"As also we have sent among you, of yourselves, a Messenger, to recite Our signs to you and to purify you, and to teach you the Book and the Wisdom ..."

(Sūrah 2: 151)

﴿و يعلمهم الكتاب والحكمة و يزكيهم ...﴾ (البقرة/ 129)

"... and teach them with the Book and the wisdom ... and purify them."

(Sūrah 2: 129)

﴿هوالذي بعث في الاميين رسولا منهم يتلوا عليهم آياته و يزكيهم و يعلمهم الكتاب والحكمة...﴾ (الجمعة/ 2)

"It is He Who has raised up among the illiterates a Messenger among themselves, to recite His signs to them, and to purify them, and to teach them the Book and the Wisdom ..."

(Sūrah 62: 2)

Muslim scholars of the past, used to recommend to their students to have spiritual training, and in seeking knowledge not to go after position, power, or wealth.

In short, in order to secure the spiritual as well as the material welfare of an Islamic society, it is essential to have learning tied with spiritual training.

5. The Holy Qur'an calls the followers of Islam a justly balanced nation:

﴿و كذلك جعلناكم امة وسطا لتكونوا شهداء علي الناس ...﴾ (البقرة/ 143)

and it recommends them to maintain equilibrium between the spiritual and the material dimensions of life:

﴿ربنا آتنا في‌الدنيا حسنة و في الآخرة حسنة ...﴾ (البقرة/ 201)

"Our Lord, grant us good in this world and good in the hereafter."

(Sūrah 2: 201)

﴿وابتغ فيما آتاك الله الدار الآخرة و لا تنسي نصيبك من الدنيا﴾ (القصص/ 77)

"And seek by means of what Allah has given you the future abode, and do not neglect your portion of this world."

(Sūrah 28: 77)

Therefore, Muslims should not, like Western people, become involved only with the material aspects of life, and should not forget the spiritual dimensions of human beings. Muslims should be aware of the fact that in Islamic outlook many material opportunities are permissible but not as an end in themselves. They serve as a ladder for the spiritual progress of man.

Muslims should never forget that Islam is radically opposed to the materialistic approach in the acquisition of science and technology and stresses that they should not be sought for their own sake. This does not in any way delimit the scope of empirical knowledge. It only means that, in making progress in this area, they should always remember God and should seek His proximity as a primary goal.

In short, today we face two realities: on the one hand we see that the West has progressed in various fields of science and technology tremendously, and on the other hand, this material progress has not brought satisfaction to the Western man. Rather, it has drawn him to the pitfall of nihilism, and in fact it has brought mankind to the verge of total annihilation. Under these circumstances, the duty of Muslims is to compensate for their lag in the fields of science and technology, and, by reviving Islamic teachings and the prevailing Islamic outlook, guide humanity towards real welfare and happiness.

III

Science and Ethics in the Qur'anic Outlook

Moral Dimension of Human Beings in the Qur'anic Outlook

In the Qur'anic outlook, science and ethics are parts of an underlying world-view which considers the phenomena of nature as signs of God, attributes a telos to the universe and assumes a moral character for the cosmos.

According to the Holy Qur'an, God endowed human beings with the capacity of understanding nature:

﴿و علّم آدم الاسماء كلها ...﴾ (البقرة/ 31)

"And He taught Adam all the names ..."

(Sūrah 2: 31)

and made them His vicegerents in the earth:

﴿و هوالذي جعلكم خلائف الأرض و رفع بعضكم فوق بعض درجات ليبلوكم في ما آتاكم انّ ربّك سريع العقاب ...﴾ (الانعام/ 165)

"It is He Who has appointed you vicegerents in the earth, and has raised some of you in ranks above others, that He may try you in what He has given you, swift is your Lord in retribution ..."

(Sūrah 6: 165)

and granted them dignity:

﴿ولقد كرّمنا بني آدم ... ﴾ (الاسراء/ 70)

"And surely We have honored the children of Adam ..."

(Sūrah 17: 70)

This was accompanied by three things:

i) Ability to use natural resources

An important by-product of human beings' knowledge of natural phenomena is their acquisition of ability to take advantage of natural resources:

﴿الم تروا انّ الله سخّر لكم ما فيالسموات و ما فيالارض و اسبغ عليكم نعمة ظاهرةً و باطنة ... ﴾ (لقمان/ 20)

"Do you not see that Allah has made what is in the heavens and what is in the earth subservient to you, and made complete to you his favors outwardly and inwardly? ..."

(Sūrah 31: 20)

ii) Individual and social responsibility

In the Qur'anic view, human beings are responsible for their actions both at the individual and the societal levels:

﴿فوربّك لنسئلنّهم اجمعين. عمّا كانوا يعلمون﴾ (الحجر/ 92-93)

"So by your Lord, we would certainly question them all, as to what they did."

(Sūrah 15: 92-93)

This responsibility includes taking care of the earth's resources as well as its environment and avoiding any kind of mischief on the earth:

﴿و لا تفسدوا في الارض بعد اصلاحها وادعوه خوفاً و طمعاً انّ رحمة الله قريب من المحسنين﴾ (الاعراف/ 56)

"And do not make any mischief in the earth after its reformation, and call on Him, fearing and hoping."

(Sūrah 7: 56)

To be more explicit, human responsibility has the following dimensions:

- responsibility of the individual towards his or her own actions:

﴿هذا يوم الفصل الذي كنتم به تكذّبون ... وقفوهم انّهم مسئولون﴾ (الصافات/ 24-21)

"This is the day for sorting things out which you have been denying … Stop them! They must be questioned."

(Sūrah 37: 21-24)

- one's responsibility towards one's society:

﴿يؤمنون بالله واليوم الآخر و يأمرون بالمعروف و ينهون عن‌المنكر و يسارعون في‌الخيرات و اولئك من الصالحين﴾ (آل‌عمران/ 114)

"They believe in God and the last day; they command decency and forbid dishonor, and compete in doing good deeds. Those are honorable people."

(Sūrah 3: 114)

and in the words of the Prophet Muhammad ﷺ:

﴿الا كلكم راع و كلكم مسئول عن رعيته﴾

"Verily, each one of you is a guardian (shepherd), and each guardian (shepherd) is responsible for his subjects (flock)." [61]

- responsibility towards other creatures:

﴿و ما من دابّة في‌الارض و لا طائر يطير بجناحيه الّا امم امثالكم ما فرّطنا في‌الكتاب من شيئ ثمّ الى ربّهم يحشرون.﴾ (الانعام/ 38)

"There is no animal crawling on the earth, nor a bird flying with its wings, but they are communities like you."

(Sūrah 6: 38)

It has been narrated from the Prophet Muhammad ﷺ:

﴿الخلق كلهم عيال‌الله، فاحبّهم الى‌الله انفعهم لعياله﴾

"All creatures are God's family (dependents); and God loves the most those who are the most beneficent to His family (dependents)." [62]

and from Imam 'Alī (AS):

﴿اتقوالله في عباده و بلاده، فانّكم مسئولون حتّي عن البقاع والبهائم﴾

"Fear God about His servants and His cities, because you will be questioned even about lands and beasts." [63]

iii) Awareness of right and wrong

According to the Qur'an, God created human beings in balance and inspired to them the good and evil:

﴿الم نجعل له عينين و لساناً و شفتين و هديناه النجدين﴾ (البلد/ 10-8)

"Have We not given him two eyes; a tongue and two lips; and shown him the two highways (of the good and the evil)?"

(Sūrah 90: 8-10)

and;

﴿و نفسٍ و ما سوّيها. فالهمها فجورها و تقويها.﴾ (الشمس/7-8)

"And by the soul and Him who shaped it and inspired it with (the knowledge) of the right and wrong."

(Sūrah 91: 7-8)

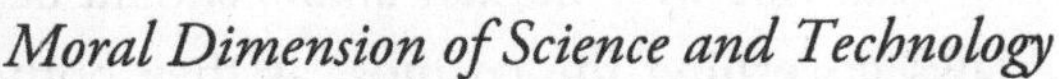

Moral Dimension of Science and Technology

There are four concepts in the Qur'an and the Islamic tradition which are relevant to the moral dimension of science and technology. These are the ideas of "useful knowledge", "balance", "purification of soul" and avoiding unsound judgments".

i) Useful knowledge

As we mentioned in the first chapter, Islam recommends the acquisition of knowledge in its generic sense. But one is supposed to seek useful knowledge. In the Prophet's words:

﴿سلو الله علماً نافعاً و تعوّذوا بالله من علم لا ينفع﴾

"Ask God for useful knowledge, and seek refuge in God from that kind of knowledge which does not benefit." [64]

Here usefulness is not used in the utilitarian sense; rather, it is in the sense of helping humankind to perform his God-assigned role in this world.

ii) Balance in the cosmos and in all human actions

In the Qur'anic view, everything in the universe is created orderly and in balance and human beings are not supposed to disturb this balance:

﴿والشمس والقمر بحسبان ... والسماء رفعها و وضعالميزان. الّا تطغوا

في الميزان﴾ (الرحمن/ 5-8)

"The sun and the moon pursue their ordered course … He raised the Heaven and set the balance. That you might not transgress the balance."

(Sūrah 55: 5-8)

This means that the laws that rule over human affairs should be harmonious with the laws governing the cosmos, as they both refer to the same God and God wants to keep everything balanced in the cosmos.

A corollary of 'balance' is the concept of "moderation". Thus, the Qur'an recommends people to avoid consuming or acquiring beyond their real needs:

﴿والذين اذا انفقوا لم يسرفوا و لم يقتروا و كان بين ذلك قواماً﴾ (الفرقان/ 67)

"And those [are servants of God] who when they spend, are neither wasteful nor niggardly, and there is a just mean between those [extremes]."

(Sūrah 25: 67)

This means that, e.g., the excessive use of natural resources is to be avoided.

iii) Purification of soul

According to the Holy Qur'an, the message of all apostles of God was two-fold: to teach people the faith and to purify them:

﴿ربّنا وابعث فيهم رسولاً منهم يتلوا عليهم آياتك و يعلّمهم الكتاب والحكمة ويزكّيهم …﴾ (البقرة/ 129)

"Our Lord! And raise up in them an apostle from among them who shall recite to them Your communications and teach them Book and the wisdom, and purify them ..."

(Sūrah 2: 129)

This means that the acquisition of knowledge has to be supplemented by the acquisition of moral values. Then the education will give direction to one's life and gives the individual a sense of responsibility. The Prophet Muhammad ﷺ, himself, mentioned that his main task had been the completion of high moral standards:

﴿انّما بعثت لاتمّم مكارم الاخلاق﴾

"Verily, I was sent out to complete high moral standards." [65]

The Qur'an recommends doing deeds that improve the well-being of an individual or a society. For example:

﴿و سارعوا الى مغفرة من ربّكم و جنةٍ عرضها السموات والارض اعدّت للمتقين. الذين ينفقون في السرّاء والضرّاء و الكاظمين الغيظ والعافين عن الناس و الله يحبّ المحسنين﴾ (آل‌عمران/ 134-133)

"And vie with one another to attain your Sustainer's forgiveness and a Paradise as vast as the heavens and the earth, which awaits the God conscious, who spend for charity in time of plenty and in time of hardship, and restrain their anger and pardon their fellow men, for God loves those who do good."

(Sūrah 3: 133-134)

iv) Avoiding unsound judgments

As we mentioned in the last chapter, the Holy Qur'an has emphasis on avoiding unsound confirmations and rejections:

﴿ولا تقف ما ليس لك به علم، انّ السمع والبصر والفؤاد كلّ اولئك كان عنه مسئولاً.﴾ (الاسراء/ 36)

"And follow not that of which you have not knowledge; surely the hearing and the sight and the heart, all of this shall be questioned about that."

(Sūrah 17: 36)

Science and Ethics in the Contemporary World

Before modern era, ethical considerations were a concern of all faithful scientists, both in the Islamic world and in the Western world. This perspective has been dramatically changed in our era and has led to grave consequences. There has been environmental pollution, excessive depletion of earth's natural resources, and the production of the worst possible kinds of mass destruction. We believe that the whole problem has developed from a change in attitude toward science that took place after the Renaissance. The progress of science has been effective in marginalizing ethical considerations and spreading around the subjectivism of moral values. This is rooted in the prevalence of a belief among scientists that facts and values are separated. They argue that science is an objective value-free enterprise dealing with facts, where as values are subjective, depending on personal opinion.

In the Qur'anic outlook, ethics is related to the world's telos, and the appropriateness of any human activity is measured by the degree of its harmony with that goal. The real ground for moral conduct is the belief in a universe which has an underlying purpose and moral order.

While we admit that on the logical basis alone one cannot derive normative statements from factual statements, we believe that science and ethics are related both at the metaphysical level and at the practical level. In the Qur'anic outlook, the study of nature and the respect for moral values both fit within the Qur'anic worldview which coordinates all aspects of human experience. Furthermore, science is a goal-directed enterprise. Thus, it must include some kinds of values that give direction to its goals, its conduct and its applications. Value-judgments enter into decision making concerning the applications of science and technology, and scientific discoveries and technological innovations often lead to important social, moral and political consequences. Thus, as a member of a society, a scientist should not ignore the consequences of his or her research or teaching.

The destructive consequences of modern science and technology has been due to the separation of facts from values and the indifference of some scientists towards the ethical and social consequences of their scientific findings or technological innovations.

To humanize applied science and technology, one needs to take into account ethical considerations, especially when one is dealing with the kind of research that affects humankind or the environment. This can be done by embedding the scientific investigation of nature within a richer framework which includes other dimensions of human experience, including spiritual and moral ones – a worldview that relates man's life to the rest of the universe. This brings us back to the Qur'anic instruction that one's scientific training should be accompanied by soul purification. This is supposed to prevent scientists from conducting any kind of research which could be harmful to the human life, other creatures and our environment.

IV

From Knowledge to Wisdom: A Qur'anic Perspective

Introduction

The unprecedented advances made during the last two hundred years in the physical and biological sciences and their technological offspring, has expanded our understanding of the world enormously and has given us tremendous control over the forces of nature and human minds. But where as these developments have brought many blessings for mankind, they have also produced many curses that threaten the whole future of human race. This is mainly due to the fact that the rise of science and technology has not been accompanied by a proper rise in human wisdom. Humanity has lost even the ancient wisdom. From the enlightenment era onwards, many scholars in the Western world have assumed that science alone, to paraphrase Nehru, can solve the problems of hunger and poverty, of insanitation and illiteracy, etc. But the events of the last century showed that science alone cannot give people self-control, kindness, or power of discounting their passions.

The loss of wisdom is mainly due to the governance of a very narrow sighted worldview that gives primacy to the sense data and neglects the spiritual dimension of humanity and the rest of the cosmos. Thus, it neglects a holistic view of reality and ignores humanity's ultimate concerns. The embedding of science within a more comprehensive framework, adds wisdom to science and that gives science a more constructive role. It also offers a coherent understanding of life, mankind and cosmos. According to this worldview, humanity is part of a wider cosmic order and is supposed to harmonize all of its activities, including the scientific and technological ones, with this cosmic order.

> *In the Qur'anic outlook, the study of nature should be for the sake of the cognition of the signs of God in the universe and for solving the individual and societal problems, without interrupting the cosmic order. Furthermore, the Holy Qur'an frequently talks of knowledge and wisdom together. In fact, the mission of the prophets is considered to be the teaching of both knowledge and wisdom to people. Only if knowledge in general, and science in particular, is subordinated to wisdom, it can bring happiness and salvation for humankind.*

The Need for the Integration of Knowledge with Wisdom

As we said the ill effects of scientific knowledge has been due to the limitations of its underlying worldview. It is for this reason that all religions of the world have urged the seekers of knowledge to augment it with wisdom. It is wisdom that helps knowledge to be used for good rather than evil, and to be a guide for life, giving it a meaning.

Characteristics of Wisdom

We begin with the definition of wisdom. According to *Oxford Companion to Philosophy*, wisdom is:

> *"A form of understanding that unites a reflective attitude and a practical concern. The aim of attitude is to understand the fundamental nature of reality and its significance for living a good life. The object of practical concern is to form a reasonable concern for good life... and to evaluate the situations in which they have to make decisions and acts from its point of view."* [66]

and *Random House College Dictionary* defines wisdom as;

> *"Knowledge of what is true or good coupled with good judgment."* [67]

Thus, wisdom has the following characteristics:

i) an inclusive framework (world view), leading to an integrative thinking and a global perspective

ii) proper use of knowledge

iii) reasoned judgment (which necessitates that crucial decisions not to be left to specialists alone, but be made by the collaboration of experts from all relevant fields

iv) recognition of the core issues (sensing what really matters and ignoring what is insignificant)

v) far sightedness (paying attention to the long-term effects and seeing how one's aims fits the ultimate goal of human life)

vi) sensitiveness to the ethical implications of one's actions

vii) appreciation of the interconnectedness of all things

and to this list I add one characteristic which is emphasized by all three monotheistic religions: God consciousness. Thus, e.g. we read in the Bible:

> *"and if you look for it [wisdom] as for silver and search for it as for hidden treasure, then you will understand the fear of the Lord and find the knowledge of God."*
>
> (Proverbs 2:4-5) [68]

and it is narrated from the Prophet Muhammad ﷺ that:

﴿رأس الحكمة مخافة الله﴾

"The peak of wisdom is fearing God." [69]

Wisdom in the Islamic Perspective

The Holy Qur'an mentions *hikmah* (wisdom) in 20 cases and in more than ten cases it is accompanied by the word "Book". Thus, e.g., we read:

> *"He it is Who raised among the illiterates an apostle among themselves, who recites to them his communications and purifies them ,and teaches them the Book and the Wisdom, although they were in clear error."*
>
> (Sūrah 62:2)

This implies that one of the main jobs of the prophets has been the instruction and propagation of wisdom. Furthermore it is said in the Qur'an that the wise are given plenty of good:

> *"He grants wisdom to whom He pleases, and whoever is granted wisdom, he is indeed given a great good ...."*
>
> (Sūrah 2: 269)

In his book on Qur'anic terms, al-Raghib al-Isfahani, defines wisdom as:

> *"Wisdom is the realization of the truth through knowledge and intellect. Thus, Wisdom in God is the Knowledge of everything and their masterful creation, and in human beings it is the performance of benevolent deeds."* [70]

and Qurashi, a contemporary Iranian author of Qur'anic terms, defines it in the following way:

> *"Wisdom is the characteristic of comprehension and diagnosis through which one can comprehend the truth and reality and*

can prevent corruption and can do one's job perfectly and masterly." [71]

In his commentary on the Holy Qur'an, the eminent Iranian Philosopher S. M. H. Tabatabai,

> *Defines wisdom as the knowledge of the origin and the hereafter, and the knowledge of natural phenomena so far as they contribute to human felicity.* [72]

To sum up, the acquisition of wisdom equips one with an understanding of some important aspects of the reality and the distinction between the truth and falsehood and between good and bad.

The Qur'an talks about God granting wisdom to Luqman (Sūrah 31:12) and then gives some samples of the wise sayings of Luqman (Sūrah 31:13-19). These include both the theoretical and the practical aspects of wisdom, including:

i) one's commitment to God and to his worship

ii) concern for the hereafter

iii) attachment to moral values , specifically moderation, humbleness and patience when confronting misfortunes

iv) consciousness of one's responsibilities towards oneself, one's family and others

v) enjoining good and forbidding bad in the society

In the Islamic outlook, the sciences of nature should be keys to our cognition of the signs of God in the universe and for solving the individual and societal problems, without interrupting the cosmic order. Furthermore, knowledge should be directed towards God. Otherwise, it could become a demonic tool which could throw humanity into an abyss.

The Qur'anic outlook for the augmentation of knowledge and wisdom is realized if an inclusive theistic worldview rules over one's mentality.

❁

Why Wisdom Is Absent in Our Era?

There several major causes for the divorce of knowledge from wisdom in our era:

1. *Narrow Specialization in Education*

   Contemporary science is content with specialization. But, due to excessive specialization in our time, there is fragmentation of knowledge both across disciplines and within disciplines. This has lead to a lack of integral vision of the individual scientists and to communities of scientists seeking their personal interest. Thus, science has become negligent about the wholeness of our environment and about the human responsibility towards the rest of the creation.

   Now, it is true that with the expansion of human knowledge there is no choice but seeking specialization. But that does not mean that one has to neglect other areas of human knowledge and the relationship of one's field of inquiry with other fields. Without a broadness of vision, the road ahead appears to be the only one worth traveling, and deprives one of having the capacity for seeing the relationship of his observations with those of other scientists in related fields. Apparently separate fields of information lead to a better understanding if they are seen within a wider context. Thus, one must embed one's specialty in a wider frame of reference. Otherwise, one will lose a unitary view of reality.

   Centers of higher learning should establish a new relationship between the natural sciences and humanities, and between all field of knowledge and human life and societal needs. This would promote human welfare and social progress.

2. *Neglect of Moral Issues in the Scientific Enterprise*

The idea of value – neutrality of science has been advertised since Hume. Thus, it is said that 'normative statements' cannot be derived from 'factual statements'. This has divorced science from moral values, and this, in turn, has led to the marginalization of ethical considerations in the scientific enterprise and has led to the spread of moral relativism in modern societies.

But the idea of the separation of facts and values is, practically speaking, a myth. Because Scientific work is not done in a human vacuum, as values outside science creep into the scientific practice at the human level. In fact, all scientific works involve some value judgments and these could be effective in the choice of theories or in the applications of science. As Popper put it:

"The fact that science cannot make any pronouncement about ethical principles has been misinterpreted as indicating that there are no such principles, while in fact the search for truth presupposes ethics." [73]

Furthermore, without a moral compass anything could result from science and its technological offspring.

Another reason for the neglect of ethical dimension in the scientific enterprise is the excessive preoccupation of scientists with their specialty and the success of the programs. As Toulmin put it:

"It was the development of specialization and professionalization that was responsible for excluding ethical issues from the foundations of science." [74]

The neglect of ethical considerations in science has loosened scientists' sense of responsibility regarding the outcome of their scientific work, and this, in turn, has contributed to the degradation of human condition on the globe. Freeman Dyson has given a good warning:

"The widening gap between technology and human needs can only be filled by ethics ... Ethics can be a force more powerful than politics and economics." [75]

3. *Thirst of Power and Success*

During the middle ages and in the early days of modern science, the pursuit of science was for the sake of contemplating God's handiwork, rather than securing material benefits for humankind. In the present secularistic context, science is sought for the control and manipulation of the nature and society. In the elegant words of E. F. Schumacher:

"The old science – 'Wisdom', or 'science for understanding' – was primarily directed 'towards the sovereign good', i.e. the True, the Good and the Beautiful, the knowledge of which would bring both happiness and salvation. The new science was directed mainly towards material power, a tendency that has meanwhile developed to such lengths that the enhancement of political and economic power is now generally taken as the first purpose of, and main justification for, expenditure on scientific work. The old science looked upon nature as God's handiwork and man's mother; the new science tends to look upon it as an adversary to be conquered or a quarry to be exploited.

The greatest and most influential difference, however, relates to the attitude of science to man. The 'science for understanding' saw man as made in the image of God, the crowning glory of creation, and hence 'in charge' of the world, because noblesse oblige. The 'science for manipulation', inevitably, sees man as nothing but an accidental product of evolution, a higher animal, a social animal, and an object for study by the same methods by which other phenomena of this world were to be studied – 'objectively'." [76]

In our era, there are two main considerations for the promotion of science and technology: 'seeking science for the sake of science' and 'seeking science for material goals and power'.

The Idea of 'science for the sake of science', however, has led to the emphasis on information gathering rather than understanding – understanding of what that information is about. Mary Midgley has put the matter nicely:

"When knowledge is ... equated with information, understanding is pushed to the background and the notion of wisdom is quite forgotten." [77]

Furthermore, with the emergence of big science, the goals of scientific and technological research are increasingly set by industry or governments whose objective is not truth but knowledge for the sake of wealth, power, and domination. It is totally forsaken that all kinds of knowledge and technology are supposed to be at the service of humanity, securing human felicity and welfare. This may require some constraints on certain areas of knowledge.

4. *Neglect of Higher Orders of Reality*

Contemporary physical science is solely based on an empiricistic approach to reality, where only the knowledge rooted in sense-data is considered as reliable. This science considers the physical world as all there is and sees no room for God in the natural order, and the spiritual dimension of human beings is ignored or denied .This has led to the confinement of human beings to the material real, with no higher aspiration than fulfilling their material needs. But, this degrades human life to that of animals, and would put human societies into unhealthy competition for material causes, with no end in sight. In the elegant words of E. F. Schumacher:

"For it is impossible for any civilization to survive without a faith in meanings and values transcending the utilitarianism of comfort and survival – in other words, without a religious faith."[78]

5. *Ultimate Questions*

A dominant outlook among contemporary scientists is that science can adequately account for everything. But, due to the limitations of its scope, science per se deals only with certain aspects of reality and cannot present a comprehensive picture of the world. It simply cannot handle moral queries, and it leaves many of the so-called ultimate questions of humanity unanswered – questions like 'What are we doing here?', 'What is the purpose of life?'. As Eugen Wigner, an eminent physicist of our era, put it:

"I don't think physics deals with everything. Whether I am happy or unhappy, whether I am afraid or fearless, whether I am noble or I am mean, how does this get represented in science? Even if there are people who would say there is a chemical imbalance, I would like to think that there is something else."[79]

These questions are concerns of all humanity, and they are meta-scientific questions. In the elegant words of Erwin Schrödinger:

"The scientific picture of the real world around me is very deficient. It gives a lot of factual information, puts all our experience in a magnificently consistent order, but it is ghastly silent about all and sundry that is really near to our heart, that really matters to us. It cannot tell us a word about red and blue, bitter and sweet, physical pain and physical delight; it knows nothing of beautiful and ugly, good or bad, God and eternity.

Science sometimes pretends to answer questions in these domains, but the answers are very often so silly that we are not inclined to take them seriously." [80]

Reflection about these questions can have lasting effects on human behavior, and on his decision making – including decisions concerning scientific enterprise.

The current scientistic worldview not only leaves all ultimate questions of human concern unanswered, it even denies the validity of such questions. Thus, the meaning of life has lost its significance, and human beings, under the overwhelming forces of technology, are demanding more and more material welfare, at the expense of their spiritual dimension. To remedy this, one has to note that scientific knowledge is not the only kind of valid knowledge and there are other areas of human knowledge that can shine light on these issues. To handle these insistent deeper issues, science must yield relevance to humanities (religion, philosophy, etc.).

Thus, there has to be a reevaluation of the present educational system in order to instill some sense of breadth in students, informing them about the interrelatedness of various disciplines. This could be done by adding sufficient number of humanity courses to the science and engineering curricula and to have across disciplinary collaborations and discussions.

Conclusion

We mentioned that scientific knowledge and its technological offspring have brought humanity a lot of blessings and curses, and that the weight of the curses threatens the future of the globe. We also echoed our view that all this is due to the divorce of knowledge from wisdom, and that this, in turn, is rooted in the prevalence a secular worldview in the academic circles. The scientists following this worldview are content with the results of their work, forgetting that science should serve humanity, rather than controlling human beings. In a theistic context, however, science is accompanied by wisdom. Thus, it is used for solving individual and societal problems - goals which lead to God's pleasure and humanity's welfare. Here, nature is viewed as a trust from God which should be handled properly. Thus, all plans for scientific progress and technological innovations should be harmonious with the cosmic order.

In my humble view, an effective way to expand the received worldview is to expand the current curricula at the institutions of higher education from the present one, which is confined to specialized training, to one that has a good touch with humanities and societal problems and includes ethical training as well.

V

Scientific Dimension of the Qur'an

In more than ten percent of the Qur'anic verses, we see references to natural phenomena. A subject of fundamental importance is to discover the kind of message that these so-called scientific verses have for us, and how we can benefit from them. There are two views about this matter.

The Qur'an as a Source of Scientific Knowledge

In our times we see many people who try to interpret some of the Qur'anic verses in the light of our present scientific knowledge. The main aim of these people is to show the miracle of the Qur'an in the scientific domain to convince non-Muslims of the glory and uniqueness of the Qur'an, and to make fellow Muslims feel proud of having such a great scripture.

But, the view of considering the Qur'an as a source of all knowledge is not a new one, and we see many great Muslim scholars of the past who were proponents of this view. One was Imam al-Ghazzali. In his book *'Ihya' 'Ulum al-Din* (The Revival of Religious Sciences), he quotes Ibn Mas'ūd as saying: "If one desires to have the knowledge of the sciences of the ancients and the moderns, he should ponder over the Qur'an." He further adds:

"In short, all sciences are included in the works and attributes of

Allah, and the Qur'an is the explanation of His essence, attributes, and works. There is no limit to these sciences, and in the Qur'an there is an indication of their confluence." [81]

In his other book *Jawahir al-Qur'an* (The Jewels of the Qur'an), which was written after the 'Ihya, Ghazzali had more to say about this matter. In the chapter on "The Stemming of the Sciences of the Ancients and the Moderns from the Qur'an", he says:

"The principle of these sciences, which we have enumerated and of those which we have not specified, are not outside the Qur'an, for all of these sciences are drawn from one of the seas of knowledge of God – may He be exalted – i.e., the sea of His works. We have already mentioned that the Qur'an is [like] a sea which as no shore, and that "if the ocean became ink for [transcribing] the words of my Lord, surely the ocean would be exhausted before the words of my Lord came to an end." Among the works of God j may he be exalted – which [for their vastness can be called] the sea of His works are, for instance, recovery and disease, as He – may He be exalted – narrating the words of Abraham, said, "When I fall ill it is He who restores me to health" ... This single work can only be known by him who knows the science of medicine completely, for this science means nothing but the knowledge of all aspects of disease together with their symptoms, and knowledge of their cure and its means. Among the works of God are [also] the determination of [man's] knowledge of the sun and the moon and of their stages according to a fixed reckoning, as God – may He be exalted – said: "The sun and the moon move according to a fixed reckoning."

"He ordained stages for the moon so that you might learn the method of calculating years and determining time ..." The real meaning of the movements of the sun and the moon according to a fixed reckoning and of the eclipses of both, of the merging of the

night into day and the manner of wrapping one of them around the other, can only be known by him who knows the manner of the composition of the heavens and the earth, and this itself is a science (i.e., astronomy) ... Should we go on narrating the details of Divine works to which the verses of the Qur'an point, it would take a long time. Only an indication of their confluence is possible [here], and we have done this where we have mentioned that knowledge of Divine works is among the sum total of knowledge of God – may He be exalted. That sum total includes these details. Likewise, every division we briefly described, will, if further divided, branch off into many details.

Reflect, then, on the Qur'an and seek its wonderful meanings, so that perchance you may encounter in it the confluence of the sciences of the ancients and the moderns and the sum total of their beginnings. Reflection on the Qur'an is intended only for reaching from the brief description of these sciences to their detailed knowledge and it is [like] an ocean that has no shore." [82]

Al-Suyuti (d. 911/1505) too, has the same view[83]. In his book *al-Itqan fi 'ulum al-Qur'an*, he tries to argue that the Qur'an contains all sciences. Using verses like:

﴿... ما فرّطنا في الكتاب من شيئ ...﴾ (الانعام/ 38)

"... We have not neglected anything in this Book ..."

(Sūrah 6: 38)

﴿... و نزّلنا عليك الكتاب تبياناً لكل شئ...﴾ (النحل/ 89)

"... And We have revealed the Book to you explaining clearly everything."

(Sūrah 16: 89)

and also prophetic traditions such as:

﴿... قال صلي الله عليه و سلم: سيكون فتن. قيل و ما المخرج منها؟ قال: كتاب الله فيه نبأ ما قبلكم و خبر ما بعدكم و ...﴾

"The Prophet said, "There shall be evils". He was asked, "What can save us from them?" he answered, "Allah's Book; there is in it the news of what happened before you and the news of what shall happen after you..."

he argues that the Qur'an contains the sciences of the ancients and the moderns. Furthermore, he says:

"Allah's Book contains everything. There is no basic section or problem of any science for which there is no indication in the Qur'an. In the Qur'an, one finds the wondrous aspects of the creatures, the spiritual dimension of the heavens and the earth, what is in the horizon's loftiest part and what is beneath the sod, the beginning of creation ..."

We find this kind of outlook in Muslim scholars of recent times too. For example, 'Abd al-Rahman al-Kawakibi (d. 1902), in his book, *Tabāyi'a al-'Istibdād* (The Nature of Despotism) says:

"In recent centuries, science has revealed many facts and these are attributed to their discoverers who are European or American. But those who examine the Qur'an carefully, find that most of those facts were stated, explicitly or implicitly, in the Qur'an thirteen centuries ago; and these were not left hidden but to show, upon their discovery a miracle of the Qur'an, and to indicate that it is the word of the Lord who is alone aware of the hidden. [84]

And among the recent proponents of this view is Mustafa Sadiq al-Rafi'ī. In the Qur'an, he said, one finds many hints for the scientific facts, and modern science helps us to interpret the meanings of some of the Qur'anic verses and to discover their facts.[85] Also Shaikh Muhammad Bakhīt says:

> *"Those who think that the Qur'an is a book for the statement of the (Islamic) laws and for legislation are avoiding the truth. The Qur'an is the source of all sciences and the human civilization .... The Qur'an, with its statements and hints, has evidence for the essence and attributes of all things and their quantitative and qualitative changes and contains all sciences dealing with the external realities, whether they are heavenly or earthly.* [86]

At this point, it is necessary to mention that the early scholar's motive in considering the Qur'an as the source of all sciences arose out of their conviction in the comprehensiveness of the Qur'an, but the recent scholars, while believing in this, have more emphasis on proving the miraculous state of the Qur'an in the scientific domain. Therefore, they try to adapt the Qur'an to the findings of contemporary science.

Some of them believe that there is nothing in the new findings of science which was not predicted by the Qur'an. For example, al-Tantawe, in his commentary on the Qur'an, tries to extract the results of the physical and natural sciences from the Qur'an, and is afraid that he might not live long enough to locate all of the findings of science and technology in the Qur'an. Yet, he is happy that the discoveries of science up to now are indicative of the prophetic power of the Qur'an.[87]

He even tries to reconcile unestablished theories of science with the Qur'an. In our time we find a tremendous increase in this kind of activity, and some Muslim scholars want to extract all the findings of contemporary science from the Qur'an, and thereby prove the miraculous nature of the Qur'an and its fitness for survival. For instance, 'Abd al-Razzāq Nawfal in his book *The Qur'an and Modern Science*, says:

> *"Thus, when we prove to non-Arabs that the Qur'an contains the*

principles of modern science and it has already spoken of every new scientific phenomenon, in this kind of miracle of the Qur'an not enough to attract their attention to the Qur'an ... Isn't the scientific miracle of the Qur'an the way to attract non-Arabs to Islam...? The day that we accomplish the translation, into various languages, of what the Qur'an has predicted and the development of various sciences has confirmed, out mission would be over and our call would be communicated, and the miraculous nature of the Qur'an would be clear for non-Arabs. [88]

And Maurice Bucaille says:

"The Qur'an follows on from the two revelations that preceded it and is not only free from contradictions in its narrations, the sign of various human manipulations to be found in the Gospels, but provide a quality all of its own for those who examine it objectively and in the light of science, i.e., its complete agreement with modern scientific data. What is more, statements are to be found in it (as has been shown) that are connected with science: and yet it is unthinkable that a man of Muhammad's time could have been the author of them. Modern scientific knowledge therefore allows us to understand certain verses of the Qur'an which, until now, it has been impossible to interpret." [89]

Some of the authors have tried very hard to extract every important idea of contemporary science from the Qur'an, and in this effort have outstretched the normal usage of the Arabic language. For example, some people claim that the idea of atom and sub-atomic particles is mentioned in the Qur'an: to prove this, they resort to the following verses: [90]

﴿... و ما يعزب عن ربك من مثقال ذرّة في الارض و لا في السماء ولا اصغر من ذلك و لا اكبر الا في كتاب مبين.﴾ (يونس/ 61)

"... there does not lie concealed from your Lord the weight of a

small particle in the earth or in the heaven, nor anything less than that nor greater, but it is in a clear Book."

(Sūrah 10: 61)

﴿ ... لا يعزب عنه مثقال ذرّة في السموات و لا في الارض و لا اصغر من ذلك و لا اكبر الا في كتاب مبين. ﴾ (سباء/ 3)

"... not the weight of a (small) particle is absent from Him in the heavens or in the earth, and neither less than that nor greater, but (all) is in a clear Book."

(Sūrah 34: 3)

Here, he identifies the Arabic word *"dharrah"* with atom, whereas the customary meaning of it was "small ant" or "a small dust particle" 12, and there is no convincing reasons to believe that Allah has used a terminology that our prophet's contemporaries could not understand.[91]

The efforts to reconcile a sacred scripture with contemporary science are not restricted to Muslims. Christians, too, try to extract modern science from the Bible, and Jews have done the same thing with the Old Testament. They, too, consider this to be a sign of validity of their book.

The Qur'an as a Book of Guidance

The aforementioned outlook towards the scientific dimension of the Qur'an has been under fire even from the old times. Abu Ishaq al-Shatibi (d. 790/1388), one of the early opponents of this view, argues that our virtuous predecessors were more knowledgeable about the Qur'an than we are, and they did not talk about these kind of sciences, and this is an indication that they did not consider the Qur'an to contain such matters.[92] Al-Shatibi relates the Qur'anic verse:

﴿ ... ما فرّطنا في الكتاب من شيئ ... ﴾ (الانعام/38)

"... we have not neglected anything in the Book ..."

(Sūrah 6: 38)

to the accountable duties and acts of worship, and identifies the word "Book" in this verse with the "Guarded Table" (mentioned in the verse 85: 22).

The aforementioned view has been criticized by some well-known scholars of recent times, too. Their argument can be summarized as follows:

1. It is not right to interpret the Qur'anic words in a way that was not known to the Arabs of the Prophet's era.
2. The Qur'an was not revealed to teach us science and technology; rather it is a book of guidance. Therefore, it is beyond its aim to talk about natural and physics sciences. The meaning of the aforementioned verses (i.e., 6:35 and 16:82) is that the Qur'an contains whatever is needed for our guidance and felicity (in this world and in the Hereafter).
3. Science has not reached its ultimate stage of progress. Therefore, it is not right to interpret the Qur'an in accordance with changeable theories. A certain theory becomes very popular during a period, and then it is replaced by another one. The Ptolemaic system was popular for a long time and them it was discarded. It is wrong to assume that the Holy Qur'an supports contradictory theories. Prominent Muslim scientists of the past, like Ibn Sina, Al-Biruni, al-Tusi, Ibn al-Haytham, ... too, did not seek scientific formulas in the Qur'an, though they had a true conviction in it and were very knowledgeable about it. Besides, if we could find the trace of all scientific theories and formulas in the Qur'an, it would not be more than a scientific encyclopedia like

other available encyclopedias. The adaptation of the Holy Qur'an to unstable theories of science has also this danger that it threatens the stability of the Qur'anic facts and opens the door for unacceptable interpretations.

4. It is Allah's will that human beings discover the secrets of nature through the use of their senses and intellect. If the Holy Qur'an contained all of the sciences of nature, human intellect would remain idle and human freedom would be meaningless. As Shaikh Muhammad 'Abduh said:

"If it were upon the Prophet to explain the natural and astronomical sciences, that would be the end of the activity of human senses and intellect, and that would spoil human freedom ... Yes, the Prophet advised people briefly to use their senses and intellect on whatever improves the welfare, broadens their knowledge, and in the end advances their souls ... Therefore, the doors for these sciences are intellect and experimentation not tradition and religious sciences." [93]

Our view

We believe that the Holy Qur'an is a book of guidance for human development, and it contains whatever human beings need in the domains of faith and action. Thus, we not do not consider it a scientific encyclopedia, neither we believe that it is right to adapt the Holy Qur'an to our changeable scientific theories. On the other hand, one cannot deny that the Qur'an contains references to some natural phenomena. But these are not for the sake of teaching science; rather, they are used as an aid in attracting people's attention to Allah's glory and to bring them closer to Him.

We also believe that the advancement of science makes it easier to understand certain Qur'anic passages. For example, the verse:

﴿ اولم يرالذين كفروا انّ السموات والارض كانتا رتقا ففتقناهما وجعلنا من الماء كل شئ حيّ ... ﴾ (الأنبياء / 30)

"Do not those who disbelieve see that the heavens and the earth were closed up, but We have opened them? And We have made of water everything living ..."

(Sūrah 21: 30)

refers to the revolution of the solar system and the role of water in life, and the verse:

﴿ و من كل شيئ خلقنا زوجين لعلكم تذكرون ﴾ (الذاريات/ 49)

"And of every We have created pairs that you might be mindful."

(Sūrah 51: 49)

informs us of the polarity evident in all creation. Modern science makes it much easier to understand this kind of verses.

In short, our view about the scientific interpretation of the Qur'an is the same as that of Shaikh Mustafa al-Maraghī, the late rector of al-Azhar University, as expressed in the introduction to Ismā'il Pāshā's *Islam and Modern Medicine*:

"It is not my intention to say that this Holy Book contains, in detail or summary, all of the sciences in the style of textbooks; rather I want to say that it contains general principles by the help of which one can derive all that is needed to know for the physical and spiritual development of human beings.

It is in fact the duty of the scientists involved with various sciences to explain for people details that are known up to their time ...

It is essential not to extend [the meaning of] a verse to such an extent that it would enable us to interpret it in the light of science. Neither one should stretch [the interpretation of] scientific facts so that one could adapt it to a Qur'anic verse. However, if the apparent meaning of a verse is consistent with an established fact, we interpret this verse with the help of that fact." [94]

If we adapt the Qur'an to philosophical schools or sciences of a period, we reach the point where, in a period of the dominance of positivism, we find a Muslim scholar trying to extract this philosophy from the Qur'an, considering it to be the basis of Qur'anic wisdom, [95] and disregarding the fact that this outlook leaves no room for metaphysics or any transcendent being. Yet, we would say that although the Qur'an is not a scientific encyclopedia, there is an important message in the verses involving natural phenomena, and Muslim scientists should focus their attention on that message rather than satisfying themselves with the miraculous aspects of the Qur'an in the scientific domain or its consistency with contemporary science.

❁

Qur'an Message for Muslim Scientists

As it is well-known, there are more than 750 Qur'anic verses dealing with natural phenomena. We think that these verses involve an important message for Muslim scientists. In our view, the following are the essential points of that message.

a) In these verses, the study of all aspects of nature and the discovery of the mysteries of creation is recommended.

﴿ و في خلقكم و ما يبث من دابّة آيات لقوم يوقنون ﴾ (الجاثيه/ 4)

"And in your creation and in what He spreads abroad of

animals there are signs for a people that are sure."

(Sūrah 45: 4)

﴿ قل انظروا ما ذا في السموات والارض ... ﴾ (يونس/ 101)

"Say, consider what is it that is in the heavens and the earth..."

(Sūrah 10: 101)

﴿قل سيروا في الارض فانظروا كيف بدء الخلق... ﴾ (العنكبوت/ 20)

"Say, travel on the earth and see how He made the first creation..."

(Sūrah 29: 20)

According to the Holy Qur'an, we have to use our senses and intellect for the understanding of nature, and this would lead us to appreciate the glory and majesty of Allah. As Allamah Tabatabā'ī puts it:

"The Qur'an invites reflection about heavenly signs, the brilliant stars and the differences in their conditions and the systematic order that governs them. It encourages meditation concerning the creation of the earth, seas, mountains, the creation of plants and animals, human beings and their inner world. Thus, it invites to a study of natural and mathematical sciences and all other fields, the learning of which is in the interest of humanity and brings felicity to human society.

The Qur'an invites to these branches of knowledge on the condition that people are guided by this knowledge of truth. Otherwise, a knowledge that serves as an amusement and hinders one from knowing God and truth is equivalent to ignorance in the vocabulary of the Qur'an." [96]

When the Holy Qur'an recommends that we look around the

earth to find out the origin of creation, this means that we have to obtain scientific facts through our efforts. It is against the spirit of the Qur'an that Muslims should remain idle while others get access to some of the mysteries of nature, and then we use their results and depend on them.

According to the Holy Qur'an, we can get access to cognition of nature if we use our senses and intellect. In fact, the main reason our great scholars, in the glorious period of Islamic civilization, paid attention to foreign (e.g., Greek) sciences was due to the Qur'an's emphasis on the study of nature.

They studied nature to discover the mysteries of creation and to become aware of Allah's wisdom and power. Al-Biruni has explicitly stated that the motive behind his research in scientific fields is Allah's words in the Qur'an:

﴿ ... و يتفكرون في خلق السموات والارض ربّنا ما خلقت هذا باطلا ...﴾ (آل‌عمران/ 191)

"... and reflect on the creation of the heavens and the earth: our Lord! You have not created this in vain ...."

(Sūrah 3: 191)

which persuades human beings to ponder about the creation of the heaven and the earth – a creation which is purposeful and not vain.

The study of the so-called scientific verses in the Qur'an should motivate Muslims to go after natural and physical sciences, and not remain content with the hints given there.

b) Some of the Qur'anic verses state that everything in this world is orderly and purposeful and there is no fault in the works of Allah:

﴿ ... و خلق كل شيئ فقدّره تقديراً ﴾ (الفرقان/ 2)

"... and He created everything, then He ordained it very exactly."

(Sūrah 25: 2)

﴿ و ما خلقنا السماء والارض و ما بينهما لاعبين ﴾ (الأنبياء / 16)

"And We did not create the heaven and the earth and what is between them for sport."

(Sūrah 21: 16)

﴿ ... ما تري في خلق الرحمن من تفاوت فارجع البصر هل تري من فطور ثم ارجع البصر كرّتين ينقلب اليك البصر خاسئاً و هو حسير ﴾ (الملك/ 3-4)

"... you see no imperfection in the creation of the beneficent God. Then look again, can you see any disorder? Then return back the eye again and again, your look shall come back to you dazzled, a weary."

(Sūrah 67: 3-4)

c) The Qur'an invites us to recognize the laws of nature (i.e., Allah's patterns in the universe) and to make use of them for the welfare of human beings, without transgressing the limits of the Sharī'ah:

﴿ الشمس والقمر بحسبان ... والسماء رفعها و وضع الميزان الا تطغوا في الميزان ﴾ (الرحمن/ 5-8)

"The sun and the moon follow reckoning .... And the heaven, He raised it high and set the balance. Transgress not the balance."

(Sūrah 55: 5-8)

Of course, the use of material means should lead to the spiritual development of human beings and not to their decay.

d) In the Qur'anic outlook, all sciences are different manifestations of a world which is created and governed by one God. Therefore, their combination should lead to a single picture of the world.

e) Lastly, one of the most important things that we learn from the Qur'an, in relation to science, is its unique world-view and epistemology. Most of the evil resulting from the growth of science has its origin in the materialistic outlook accompanying modern science. The Qur'an warns us against these pitfalls and informs us of the impediments to correct cognition of nature. It teaches us what tools to use for the cognition of nature and what prevents us from using those tools properly.

In short, we believe that the most important lessons we learn from the so-called scientific verses of the Qur'an are:

1. Priority should be given to the discovery of nature, using human senses and intellect.
2. The Holy Qur'an can give us the correct world-view.
3. Some of the Qur'anic verses may inspire scientists to do certain experimental or theoretical works.

VI

Philosophy of Science: A Qur'anic Approach

The Aim of Understanding Nature

Nature means the physical world, that is, the world with which we come into contact through our senses In the Holy Qur'an, there are more than 750 verses in reference to natural phenomena. In most of these verses, the study of the book of creation and the meditation upon its contents has been recommended. As confirmed by many outstanding Islamic scholars, the Qur'an is not a book of natural science, but rather one of guidance and enlightenment. The Qur'anic reference to the natural phenomena is meant to call man's attention to the might and glory of the Wise Creator of the universe through quest and meditation upon natural beings and to encourage him to strive to be in close proximity to Him.

From the Qur'anic viewpoint, natural phenomena are signs of the Almighty, and through the understanding of signs we attain cognition of the Lord of signs:

﴿و من آياته ان خلق لكم من انفسكم ازواجاً لتسكنوا اليها و جعل بينكم مودّة و رحمة، انّ في ذلك لآيات لقوم يتفكرون﴾ (الروم/ 21)

"And one of the signs is that He created mates for you from yourselves that you may find rest in them, and He put between

you love and compassion, most surely there are signs in this for a people who reflect."

(Sūrah 30: 21)

﴿و من آياته يريكم البرق خوفاً و طمعاً و ينزل من السماء ماء فيحيى بهالارض بعد موتها انّ في ذلك لآيات لقوم يعقلون﴾ (الروم/ 24)

"And one of His signs is that He shows you the lightening for fear and for hope and sends down water form the cloud, then gives life therewith to the earth after its death; most surely there are signs in this for a people who understand."

(Sūrah 30: 24)

﴿و من آياته خلق السموات والارض و اختلاف السنتكم و الوانكم، انّ في ذلك لآيات للعالمين﴾ (الروم/ 22)

"And one of His signs is the creation of the heavens and the earth and the diversity of your tongues and colour; most surely there are signs in this for the learned."

(Sūrah 30: 22)

From the Qur'anic viewpoint, the cognition of nature is not a fruitful undertaking except when it helps us to understand the Wise Creator of this world and to attain close proximity to Him. Understanding nature can promote man's insight towards the cognition of Allah and enables him to better utilize the gifts of Allah for his own eternal felicity and well-being.

The Possibility of Understanding Nature

In the Qur'an, there are many verses inviting man to study nature:

﴿و قل انظروا ماذا في السموات والأرض ...﴾ (يونس/ 101)

"Say: Consider what is it that is in the heavens and the earth..."

(Sūrah 10: 101)

﴿و في الارض آيات للموقنين و في انفسكم افلا تبصرون﴾ (الذاريات/ 20-21)

"And in the earth there are signs for those who are sure; And in your own souls (too); will you not then see?"

(Sūrah 51: 20-21)

﴿قل سيروا في الارض فانظروا كيف بدأالخلق ...﴾ (العنكبوت/ 20)

"Say: Travel on the earth and see how He made the first creation."

(Sūrah 29: 20)

﴿فلينظر الانسان ممّ خلق ...﴾ (الطارق/ 5)

"So let man consider of what he is created."

(Sūrah 86:5)

These verses show that understanding nature is possible, otherwise God would have not recommended its study.

From the following verses, too, we realize that man has been endowed with the talent of cognition, and he has to exploit this- faculty to the best of his ability:

﴿و علم آدم الاسماء كلها ...﴾ (البقره/ 31)

"And He taught Adam all the names."

(Sūrah 2: 31)

﴿علّم الانسان ما لم يعلم﴾ (العلق/ 5)

"Taught man what (he) knew not."

(Sūrah 96: 5)

﴿والله اخرجكم من بطون امّهاتكم لاتعلمون شيئاً و جعل لكم السمع و الابصار والافئدة لعلّكم تشكرون﴾ (النحل/ 78)

"And Allah has brought you from the wombs of your mothers - you did not know anything - and He gave you the hearing and the sight and the hearts that you give thanks."

(Sūrah 16: 78)

Moreover, the Qur'an promises that the world is comprehensible:

﴿سنريهم آياتنا في الآفاق و في انفسهم حتّي يتبيّن لهم انّه الحق ...﴾ (فصلت/ 53)

"We will soon show them Our signs in the universe and in their own souls, so that it becomes clear unto them that He is indeed the truth."

(Sūrah 41: 53)

﴿و قل الحمدلله سيريكم آياته فتعرفونها و ما ربك بغافل عمّا تعملون﴾ (النمل/ 93)

"And say: praise be to Allah, He will show you His signs so that you shall recognize them; nor is your Lord heedless of what you do."

(Sūrah 27:93)

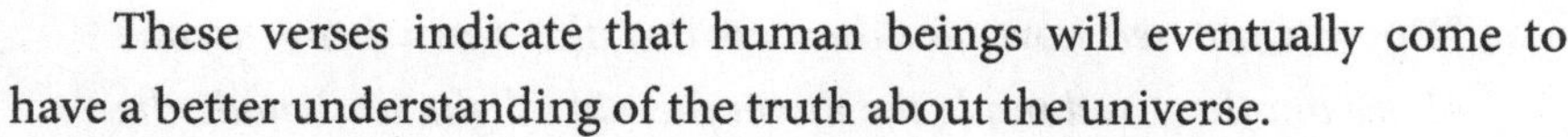

These verses indicate that human beings will eventually come to have a better understanding of the truth about the universe.

❁

The Main Issues In Understanding Nature

Although from the viewpoint of the Qur'an, the ultimate goal in understanding nature is to comprehend and approach God, yet there are certain subsidiary goals, the apprehension of which may be considered as preliminary steps towards that ultimate goal.

There are certain issues involving natural phenomena, which are pointed out in the Holy Qur'an. Here, we classify them into three groups:

1. Origin and evolution of beings and phenomena

There are verses that indicate that we should attempt to discover the origin and evolution of beings, as this will help in enhancing man's faith and in bringing him closer to God.

﴿اولم يرالذين كفروا انّ السموات والارض كانتا رتقاً ففتقناهم و جعلنا من الماء كلّ شيئ حيّ ...﴾ (الانبياء / 30)

"Do those who disbelieve not see that the heavens and the earth were closed up, but We have opened them, and have made of water everything living ..."

(Sūrah 21: 30)

﴿الم تروا كيف خلق الله سبع السموات طباقاً و جعل القمر فيهن نوراً و جعل الشمس سراجاً﴾ (نوح/ 16-15)

"Do you not see how God has created the seven heavens one above another, and made the moon therein a light, and made the sun a lamp?"

(Sūrah 71: 15-16)

﴿الذي احسن كل شيئ خلقه و بدأ خلق الانسان من طين ثم جعل نسله من سلالة من ماء مهين ثم سوّيه و نفخ فيه من روحه و جعل لكم السمع والابصار والافئدة قليلاً ما تشكرون﴾ (السجدة/ 9-7)

"Who made good everything that He has created, and He began the creation of man from dust. Then He made his progeny of an extract of water held in light estimation. Then He made him complete and breathed into him of His spirit and made for you the earth, and the air and the hearts. Little is it that you give thanks."

(Sūrah 32: 7-9)

﴿افلا ينظرون الي الابل كيف خلقت و الي السماء كيف رفعت و الي الجبال كيف نصبت و الي الارض كيف سطحت﴾ (الغاشيه/ 20-17)

"Will they not then consider the camels, how they are created and the heaven, how it is reared aloft, and the mountains, how they are firmly fixed, and the earth, how it is made a vast expanse?"

(Sūrah 88: 17-20)

In some verses of the Qur'an, certain natural phenomena are mentioned as indications of the Resurrection:

﴿اوليس الذي خلق السموات والارض بقادر علي ان يخلق مثلهم بلي و هو الخلاق العليم﴾ (يس/ 81)

"Is not He Who created the heavens and the earth, able to create the like of them? Yes! And He is the Creator (of All), the Knower."

(Sūrah 36: 81)

﴿والله الذي ارسل الرياح فتثير سحابا فسقناه الى بلد ميّت فاحيينا به الارض بعد موتها كذلك النشور﴾ (فاطر/ 9)

"And God is He Who sends the winds so they rise a cloud, then we drive it on to a dead country, and therewith we give life to the earth after its death, even so is the uprising."

(Sūrah 35: 9)

﴿يا ايّهاالناس ان كنتم في ريب من البعث فانّا خلقناكم من تراب ثم من نطفة ثم من علقة ... و تري الارض هامدة فاذا انزلنا عليها الماء اهتزّت و ربت وانبتت من كل زوج بهيج﴾ (الحج/ 5)

"O People! If you are in doubt about the Resurrection, then surely We created you from dust, then from a small life-germ, then from a clot, then from a lump of flesh, complete in make and incomplete ... and you see the earth's sterile land, but when We send down on it the water, it stirs and swells and brings forth of every kind a beautiful herbage."

(Sūrah 22: 5)

2. The discovery of order, co-ordination and purpose

Many of the verses in the Qur'an mention the existence of order, co-ordination, and purpose in nature as evidences confirming the existence of the Wise, Omniscient Creator. These verses can be classified into several groups:

a) Some verses specify that the creation of the heavens and the earth was not in vain, but had indeed some purpose behind it. For example:

﴿و هو الذي خلق السموات والارض بالحق ...﴾ (الانعام/ 73)

"And He it is Who has created heavens and the earth in truth..."

(Sūrah 6: 73)

﴿و ما خلقنا السماء والارض و ما بينهما لاعبين﴾ (الأنبياء / 16)

"And We did not create the heaven and the earth and what is between them for sport."

(Sūrah 21: 16)

﴿افحسبتم انّما خلقناكم عبثاً وانكم الينا لا ترجعون﴾ (المؤمنون/ 115)

"What! Did you then think that We had created you in vain and that you shall not be returned to Us?"

(Sūrah 23: 115)

b) It is mentioned in some verses that events follow a natural course for a certain pre-determined period:

﴿اولم يتفكروا في انفسهم ما خلق الله السموات والارض و ما بينهما الا بالحق واجل مسمّي و انّ كثيراً من الناس بلقاء ربهم لكافرون﴾ (الروم/ 8)

"Do they not reflect within themselves: Allah did not create the heaven and the earth and what is between them but in truth, and (for) an appointed term? And most surely most of the people are deniers of the meeting of their Lord."

(Sūrah 30: 8)

﴿الله الذي رفع السموات بغير عمد ترونها ثم استوي علي العرش و سخّر الشمس و القمر كل يجري لاجل مسمّي يدبّر الامر يفصّل الآيات لعلكم بلقاء

ربكم توقنون﴾ (الرعد/ 2)

"Allah, He who raised the heaves without any pillars that you see, and He is firm in power, and He made the sun and the moon subservient (to you); each one pursues its course to an appointed time; He regulates the affair, making clear the signs that you may be certain of meeting your Lord."

(Sūrah 13: 2)

c) Some verses tell us that the whole process of creation and the course of events in nature follow a proper reckoning and measure (that is, for everything there is a definite size and measure):

﴿والشمس والقمر بحسبان﴾ (الرحمن/ 5)

"The sun and moon follow a reckoning."

(Sūrah 55: 5)

﴿و انّ من شيئ الّا عندنا خزائنه و ما ننزّله الّا بقدر معلوم﴾ (الحجر/ 21)

"And there is not a thing but with Us are the treasures of it, and We do not send it down but in a known measure."

(Sūrah 15: 21)

﴿و كل شيئ عنده بمقدار﴾ (الرعد/8)

"And there is a measure with Him of everything."

(Sūrah 13: 8)

﴿و خلق كل شيئ فقدّره تقديراً﴾ (الفرقان/ 2)

"... He created everything then ordained for it a measure."

(Sūrah 25: 2)

﴿والسماء رفعها و وضع الميزان﴾ (الرحمن/ 7)

"And the heaven, He raised it high and He made the balance."

(Sūrah 55: 7)

﴿و أنبتنا فيها من كل شيئ موزون﴾ (الحجر/ 19)

"... And caused to grow in it of every suitable thing."

(Sūrah 15: 19)

It is precisely for the very existence of this order that laws of nature become significant. The scholars of natural science would not have so ardently pursued the discovery of these laws had they not been subconsciously aware of this very natural order. From the above-mentioned verses and those ensuing, one can conclude that the discovery of order and coordination in nature (i.e. the laws of nature) and the certitude of God's handiwork is of great significance in understanding nature:

﴿هوالذي جعل الشمس ضياء والقمر نوراً و قدّره منازل لتعلموا عدد السنين والحساب ما خلق الله ذلك الا بالحق يفصّل الآيات لقوم يعلمون﴾ (يونس/ 5)

"He it is who made the sun a shining brightness and the moon a light, and ordained for it mansions that you might know the computation of years and reckoning. God did not create it but in truth; He makes the signs manifest for people who know."

(Sūrah 10: 5)

﴿... ما تري في خلق الرحمن من تفاوت فارجع البصر هل تري من فطور﴾ (الملك/ 3)

"... You see no congruity in the creation of the Beneficent God; then look again, can you see any disorder?"

(Sūrah 67: 3)

3. Making legitimate uses of the means provided by God (for human beings)

In a good number of verses God mentions the gifts He has granted man:

﴿و سخّر لكم ما في السموات و ما في الارض جميعاً ...﴾ (الجاثية/ 13)

"And He has made subservient to you whatsoever is in the heavens and whatsoever is in the earth."

(Sūrah 45: 13)

﴿ولقد مكناكم في الارض و جعلناكم فيها معايش قليلاً ما تشكرون﴾ (الاعراف/ 10)

"And certainly We have established you in the earth and made in it means of livelihood for you, little it is that you give thanks."

(Sūrah 7: 10)

﴿و من رحمته جعل لكم الليل والنهار لتسكنوا فيه ولتبتغوا من فضله ولعلكم تشكرون﴾ (القصص/ 73)

"And out of His mercy He has made for you the night and day that you may rest therein, and that you seek of His grace and that you give thanks."

(Sūrah 28: 73)

﴿و من آياته انّ يرسل الرياح مبشرات وليذيقكم من رحمته و لتجري الفلك بامره ولتبتغوا من فضله ولعلكم تشكرون﴾ (الروم/ 46)

"And one of His signs is that He sends forth the winds bearing good news and that He may make you taste of His mercy, and

that the ships may run by His command, and that you may seek of His grace, and that you may be grateful."

(Sūrah 30: 46)

﴿و هوالذي جعل لكم النجوم لتهتدوا بها في الظلمات البّر و البحر قد فصّلنا الآيات لقوم يعلمون﴾ (الانعام/ 97)

"And He it is who has made the stars for you, that you might follow the right way thereby in the darkness of the land and the sea, truly We have made plain the signs for a people who know."

(Sūrah 6: 97)

In these verses, the reason for reminding man of Allah's blessings is to make him familiar with them, to urge him to use them, and to offer his thanks to Allah. Thanksgiving means to use God's blessings in the appropriate way for which they have been bestowed by the Almighty. It is thus important for the believer to make a conscientious use of Allah's bounties, leading his society towards eternal felicity. Hence technology, which is the practical use of natural means, will be instrumental in realizing Divine goals.

❁

Ways of Understanding Nature

Some Qur'anic verses tell us about the ways of understanding nature. We begin our discussion with the glorious verse:

﴿والله اخرجكم من بطون امهاتكم لاتعلمون شيئاً وجعل لكم السمع والابصار والافئدة ...﴾ (النحل/ 78)

"And God has brought you forth from the wombs of your mothers –you did not know anything – and He gave you the

hearing and the sight and the heart..."

(Sūrah 16: 78)

It says that understanding is attained through eyes, ears and intellect. Here, from amongst external senses, only sight and hearing have been mentioned, because they are the main tools with the help of which one acquires knowledge of the physical world. However, one can deduce from the Holy Qur'an that the senses of taste, smell, and touch are also useful in giving us valuable information about the external world, Here we quote three verses:

﴿... فلما **ذاقا** الشجرة بدت لهما سؤاتهما وطفقا يخصفان عليهما من ورق الجنة ...﴾ (الاعراف/ 22)

"So when they tasted of the tree, their shameful parts became manifest to them, and they both began to cover themselves with the leaves of the garden ..."

(Sūrah 7: 22)

﴿و لما فصلت العير قال ابوهم انّي **لاجد ريح** يوسف لولا ان تفندون﴾ (يوسف/ 94)

"And when the caravan had departed, their father said: Most surely I ***smell*** *the scent of Yūsuf [Joseph], unless you pronounce me to be weak in judgement."*

(Sūrah 12: 94)

﴿ولو نزّلنا عليك كتاباً في قرطاس **فلمسوه** بايديهم لقال الذين كفروا انّ هذا سحر مبين﴾ (الانعام/ 7)

"And if we had sent to you a writing on a paper, then they had ***touched*** *it with their hands, certainly those who disbelieve would have said: This is nothing but clear enchantment."*

(Sūrah 6: 7)

The word *Fuw'ād* has been interpreted as a means of perception and reasoning.[97] Heart has also been mentioned as means of understanding and perception:

﴿ افلم يسيروا في الارض فتكون لهم قلوب يعقلون بها ... ﴾ (الحج/ 46)

"Have they not traveled in the land so that they should have hearts with which to understand?"

(Sūrah 22: 46)

﴿ ... لهم قلوب لايفقهون بها ... ﴾ (الاعراف/ 179)

"... They have hearts with which they do not understand ..."

(Sūrah 7:179)

﴿ ... و طبع علي قلوبهم فهم لا يفقهون ﴾ (التوبه/ 87)

"And a seal is set on their hearts so they do not understand."

(Sūrah 9: 87)

﴿ ... انّ في ذلك لذكري لمن كان له قلب ... ﴾ (ق/ 37)

"Most surely there is a reminder in this for him who has a heart."

(Sūrah 50: 37)

﴿ اولئك الذين طبع الله علي قلوبهم و سمعهم و ابصارهم و اولئك هم الغافلون ﴾ (النحل/ 108)

"These are they on whose hearts and hearing and eyes God has set a seal and these are the heedless ones."

(Sūrah 16: 108)

In many Islamic tradition, too, "heart" has been used as a tool of reasoning. It has been cited by Imam al-Sādiq (AS) that:

﴿فمنها قلبه الذي به يعقل و يفقه و يفهم ...﴾

"Among his organs is his heart which is the means of reasoning, perception and comprehension." [98]

It is also quoted from Imam 'Alī Ibn Muhammad al-Hādī (AS):

﴿دلّ القرآن و اخبار الرسول (ص) انّ القلب مالك لجميع الحواس يصحح افعالها و لا يبطل مايصحح القلب شيئ﴾

"The Qur'an and the traditions of the Prophet ﷺ indicate that 'heart' is the lord of all senses, and coordinates their deeds (functions); and whatever heart sets right nothing can spoil." [99]

Through the verses of the Qur'an, we intend to deduce that the channels through which we understand nature are:

1. External senses (by means of which observation and experimentation take place)
2. Intellect, unpolluted of vices (dominant over desires and fancies, and free from blind imitation)
3. Revelation, and inspiration.

1. The role of observation and reasoning in understanding nature

There are a number of verses in the Holy Qur'an that encourage man to use his senses in search of truth. Here are some examples of those verses:

﴿قل سيروا في الارض فانظروا كيف بدأالخلق ...﴾ (العنكبوت/ 20)

"Say: Travel on the earth and see how He made the first creation."

(Sūrah 29: 20)

﴿قل انظروا ما ذا في السموات والارض ...﴾ (يونس/ 101)

"Say: Consider what is it that is in the heavens and the earth."

(Sūrah 10: 101)

﴿افلا ينظرون الى الابل كيف خلقت﴾ (الغاشيه/ 17)

"Will they then consider the camels, how they are created?"

(Sūrah 88: 17)

﴿اولم يروا الى الارض كم انبتنا فيها من كل زوج كريم﴾ (الشعراء/ 7)

"Do they not see the earth, how many of every noble kind We have caused to grow in it?"

(Sūrah 26: 7)

In these verses, observation and seeing (vision) imply "seeing with the help of right reasoning"[100]. In a number of cases certain practical experiments are mentioned as means for acquiring knowledge. We are going to cite three examples of them:

a) Through a crow, Allah teaches Cain how to bury a dead body:

﴿فبعث الله غرابا يبحث في الارض ليريه كيف يواري سوأة اخيه قال يا ويلتي اعجزت ان اكون مثل هذا الغراب فاواري سواة اخي فاصبح من النادمين﴾ (المائده/ 31)

"Then God sent a crow, digging the earth, so that He might show him (Cain) how he should cover the dead body of his brother. He said: Woe, me! Do I lack the strength that I should be like a crow and cover the dead body of my brother? So he became of those who regret."

(Sūrah 5: 31)

b) God teaches the qualified man the possibility of giving new life to the dead:

﴿او كالذي مرّ علي قَرية و هي خاوية علي عروشها قال أنّي يحيي هذه الله بعد موتها فأماته الله مائة عام ثم بعثه قال كم لبثت قال لبثت يوما او بعض يوم قال بل لبثت مائة عام فانظر الى طعامك و شرابك لم يتسنّه وانظر الى حمارك و لنجعلك آية للناس وانظر الى العظام كيف ننشزها ثم نكسوها لحما فلما تبين له قال اعلم انّ الله علي كل شيئ قدير﴾ (البقرة/ 259)

"Or the like of him who passed by a town, and it had fallen down upon its roofs; he said; When will Allah give it life after its death? So Allah caused him to die for a hundred years, then raised him to life. He said:' How long have you tarried?' He said (in reply):'I have tarried a day, or part of a day.' Said He: ' Nay! You have tarried a hundred years; then look at your ass and that We may make you a sign to men, and look at the bones, how we set them together, then clothed them with flesh'; so when it became clear to him, he said: 'I know that Allah has power over all things'."

(Sūrah 2: 259)

c) God shows 'Ibrāhīm (Abraham) how He gives life to the dead:

﴿و اذ قال ابراهيم رب ارني كيف تحيي الموتي قال اولم نؤمن قال بلي ولكن ليطمئنّ قلبي قال فخذ اربعة من الطير فصرهن اليك ثم اجعل علي كل جبل منهن جزءاً ثم ادعهن ياتينك سعيا واعلم انّ الله عزيز حكيم﴾ (البقرة/ 260)

"And when 'Ibrāhīm [Abraham] said: 'My Lord show me how Thou givest life to the dead', He said: 'What! And do you not believe?' He said: 'Yes, that my heart may be at ease.' He said:' Then take four of the birds, then train them to follow you, then place on every mountain a part of them, then they will come to you flying; and know that Allah is Mighty, Wise'."

(Sūrah 2: 260)

Besides there are many tangible parables in the Qur'an which are meant to teach one something perceptible:

﴿و مثل كلمة خبيثة كشجرة خبيثة اجتثت من فوق الارض مالها من قرار﴾ (ابراهيم/ 26)

"And the parable of an evil word is as an evil tree pulled up from the earth's surface; it has no stability."

(Sūrah 14:26)

﴿الله نورالسموات والارض مثل نوره كمشكوة فيها مصباح المصباح في زجاجة الزجاجة كانّها كوكب دّري يوقد من شجرة مباركة زيتونة لاشرقية و لاغربية يكاد زيتها يضيء ولولم تمسسه نار نور علي نور يهدي‌الله لنوره من يشاء ...﴾ (النور/ 35)

"Allah is the light of the heavens and the earth; a likeness of his light is as a niche in which is a lamp, the lamp is in a glass, (and) the glass is as it were a brightly shining star, lit from a blessed olive-tree, neither eastern nor western, the oil whereof almost gives light though fire touch it not - light upon light - Allah guides to his light whom He pleases..."

(Sūrah 24:35)

﴿والله الذي ارسل الرياح فتثير سحاباً فسقناه الى بلد ميت فاحيينا به الارض بعد موتها كذلك النشور﴾ (فاطر/ 9)

"And God is He Who sent the winds so they rise a cloud, then We drive it on to a dead country and therewith We give life to the earth after death, even so is the quickening."

(Sūrah 35: 9)

Therefore, there is no doubt that the Qur'an considers external senses the primary tools in getting a part of our knowledge; but both in the above verses, and in many others to come, sensory stimuli have not been suggested as the sole means of nature's cognition. In order to substantiate this claim we can advance the following arguments:

1. In most of the Qur'anic verses, wherever natural phenomena are mentioned, it is explicitly pointed out that the perception of Divine signs in nature and their relation to the Lord of signs is within the reach of men of intellect, capable of reflection. Here are a few examples of such verses:

﴿هوالذي انزل من السماء ماءً لكم منه شراب و منه شجر فيه تسيمون ينبت لكم به الزرع والزيتون والنخيل والاعناب و من كل الثمرات انّ في ذلك لاية لقوم يتفكرون﴾ (النحل/ 11-10)

"He it is who sends down water from the heaven (cloud) for you, it gives drink, and by it (grow) the trees upon which you pasture. He causes to grow for you thereby herbage, and the olives and the palm trees, and the grapes and of all the fruits, most surely there is a sign in this for a people who reflect."

(Sūrah 16: 10-11)

﴿و هوالذي جعل لكم النجوم لتهتدوا بها في ظلمات البرّ والبحر، قد فصّلنا الايات لقوم يعلمون﴾ (الانعام/ 97)

"And He it is Who made the stars for you that you that you might follow the right way thereby in the darkness of the land and the sea. Truly we have made plain the signs for a people who know."

(Sūrah 6: 97)

﴿و سخّركم الليل والنهار والشمس والقمر والنجوم مسخرات بامره انّ في ذلك لآيات لقوم يعقلون﴾ (النحل/ 12)

"And He has made subservient for you the night and the day and the sun and the moon and the stars are subservient by His commandment; most surly there are signs these for a people who ponder."

(Sūrah 16: 12)

﴿و من كل شيئ خلقنا زوجين لعلكم تذكرون﴾ (الذاريات/ 49)

"And of everything we have created pairs that you may be mindful."

(Sūrah 51: 49)

﴿و هوالذي أنشأكم من نفس واحدة فمستقر و مستودع قد فصّلنا الآيات لقوم يفقهون﴾ (الانعام/ 98)

"And He it is Who has brought you into you into being from a single, then there is (for you) a resting place and a depository indeed. We have made plain the signs for a people who understand."

(Sūrah 6: 98)

The use of such words as "*tafakkur, ta'aqqull* and *tafaqquh* ..." in the above verses indicate (with different shades of emphasis) that to understand nature, one should make use of one's intellect. The word *tafakkur* (meditation) in many of the verses means reflection on existing information and moving towards fresh awareness. [101]

a) The words *Ta'aqqull* and *Tafaqquh* show the intellectual advancement. Therefore the cognition that originates through the senses should be backed by reflection and reasoning in order to enhance our knowledge. The following quotations from Imam al-Sādiq (AS) confirm this point:

﴿انّ اول الامور و مبدأها و قوتها و عمارتها التي لاينتفع بشيئ الا به، العقل الذي جعله الله زينة لخلقه و نوراً لهم، فبالعقل عرف العباد خالقهم، و انهم مخلوقون، انّه المدبّر لهم و انهم المدبرون ... و استدلوا بعقولهم علي ما رأوا من خلقه، و من سمائه و ارضه، و شمسه و قمره، وليله و نهاره، و بانّ له و لهم خالقاً و مدبّراً لم يزل و لايزول، و عرفوا به الحسن من القبيح، و ان الظلمة في الجهل، و ان النور في العلم، فهذا ما دلهم عليه العقل﴾

"The origin and commencement of everything, and the cause of their flourishing, is the intellect without which nothing can be achieved. God has endowed His servants with the light and ornament of intellect. By means of intellect the servants know their Creator and get to understand that He is the Ruler and they are under His rule, He is immortal and they are mortal. Their intellect directs them to infer through the observation of the Handiwork of God such as the heavens, the earth, the sun, the moon, the day and night ... –That there is a Creator and Controller of all these beings, and He has always been and will exist forever. It is through the intellect that man recognizes grace from disgrace, and realizes that light is associated with knowledge, and ignorance bears darkness. This inference can be made only through the intellect." [102]

b) Shaikh Mufīd, in his book *al-'Irshād'* narrates that Abū Shākir Daysāni said to Imam al-Sādiq (AS):

"You know that we do not accept anything unless we see, hear, taste, smell or feel it with our senses".

Imam al-Sādiq (AS) answered:

﴿ذكرت الحواس الخمس و هي لاتنفع في الاستنباط الا بدليل، كما لاتقطع الظلمة بغير مصباح﴾

"You mentioned the five senses, but they never find the truth unless their findings are steered through the channel of intellect, in the same manner as darkness cannot be removed except with a lamp." [103]

c) There is another quotation from Imam al-Sādiq (AS) which says:

﴿فانك لو رأيت حجراً يرتفع في الهواء، علمت انّ رامياً رمي به، فليس هذا العلم من قبل البصر، بل من قبل العقل، لانّ العقل هوالذي يميّزه، فيعلم انّ الحجر لايذهب علواً تلقاء نفسه ...﴾

"When you see a stone moving upwards in the air, you know that some person has thrown it. This knowledge has not come to you through your eyes, but through the channel of intellect, because it is intellect which infers that a stone cannot go up in the air by itself." [104]

Therefore, it can be concluded that though observation and experimentation are indispensable for obtaining information from the external world, they are not a sufficient means. Should we rely solely on external senses, we will not be able to interpret the physical world, and find the relation between natural events. In fact, man is no different from other animals as far as external senses are concerned, and some of the animals in this respect, are even better equipped than human beings. What distinguishes man from animals is his talent for profound observation of the world and the interpretation of events. And this is due to a faculty called rational faculty, which is capable of relating the signs and symbols attained through the senses, and then interpreting them. Senses give us a series of isolated signs and symbols, and intellect discovers their inter-relationship.

2. In the Qur'an, there are many verses denoting that in some people, eyes, ears and heart do not perform their roles, and while

seeing the Almighty's signs in nature, they do not meditate on them, nor do they benefit from those (blessings):

﴿و كايّن من آية في السموات والارض يمرّون عليها وهم عنها معرضون﴾ (يوسف/ 105)

"And how many a sign in the heavens and the earth they pass by, yet they turn aside from it."

(Sūrah 12: 105)

﴿... لهم قلوب لايفقهون بها و لهم اعين لايبصرون بها و لهم آذان لايسمعون بها ...﴾ (الاعراف/ 179)

"They have hearts with which they do not understand, and they have eyes with which they do not see, and they have ears with which they do not hear ..."

(Sūrah 7: 179)

﴿... ام لهم اعين يبصرون بها ام لهم آذان يسمعون بها ...﴾ (الاعراف/ 195)

"... Or have they eyes with which they see, or have they ears with which they hear...?"

(Sūrah 7: 195)

﴿ولا تكونوا كالذين قالوا سمعنا و هم لايسمعون﴾ (الانفال/ 21)

"And be not like those who said, 'we hear', and they did not hear."

(Sūrah 8: 21)

﴿و ان تدعوهم الى الهدي لايسمعوا و تريهم ينظرون اليك و هم لايبصرون﴾(الاعراف/ 198)

"And if you invite them to guidance, they do not hear, and you see them looking towards you, yet they do not see."

(Sūrah 7: 198)

﴿افلم يسيروا في الارض فتكون لهم قلوب يعقلون بها او آذان يسمعون بها فانها لا تعمي الابصار ولكن تعمي القلوب التي في الصدور﴾ (الحج/ 46)

"Have they not traveled in the land so that they should have hearts with which to understand, or ears with which to hear? For surely it is not eyes that are blind, but blind are the hearts which are in the breasts."

(Sūrah 22: 46)

It is quoted from our great Prophet Muhammad ﷺ that:

﴿ليس الاعمي من يعمي بصره، انما الاعمي من تعمي بصيرته﴾

"Blind is not a person who lacks eyes, but the one who lacks insight," [105]

Some people, interpreting the above verses, rightly say that we have two kinds of sight and hearing – the physical or external and spiritual or internal ones. The external organs of sight and hearing are tools for perception, and the internal ones serve for the appropriate use of those tools.

Fakhr al-Dīn Rāzī refers to the following verse:

﴿مثل الفريقين كالاعمي والأصم والبصير ...﴾ (هود/ 24)

"The likeness of the two parties is as that of the blind and the deaf."

(Sūrah 11: 24)

and says:

"There is a similarity in the creation of body and spirit; that is, both have eyes and ears. In the same way that a deaf and blind person, in absolute silence and darkness, finds himself at a loss, an astray, irreligious and ignorant person's heart, too, lacks the power o f sight and hearing and he is lost in wilderness." [106]

We would rather interpret the above verses in this way: that eyes, ears and other external senses are means for the intellect, and their acquisitions could be complete and meaningful if they go through the channel of the intellect. Eyes see, but the intellect interprets the result of sight and issues the verdict.[107] The function of sight can be considered complete when it goes with insight, i.e., when sensory perception is supplemented with (supra-sensory) intellect. Here are a few verses confirming this interpretation:

﴿افانت تسمع الصّم ولو كانوا لا يعقلون﴾ (يونس/ 42)

"But can you make the deaf to hear though they will not understand?"

(Sūrah 10: 42)

﴿ولا تكونوا كالذين قالوا سمعنا و هم لايسمعون ان شرّالدواب عندالله الصم البكم الذين لايعقلون﴾ (الانعام/21-22)

"And be not like those who said, 'we hear', and they did not hear. Surely the vilest of animals in Allah's sight are the deaf, the dumb, who do not understand."

(Sūrah 8: 21-22)

It has been quoted from Imam 'Alī (AS) in *Nahj al-Balāghah*:

﴿فانّما البصير من سمع فتفكر ونظر فابصر، وانتفع بالعبر ثم سلك جدداً

واضحاً و تجنب الصرعه في المهاوي والضلال في المغاوي﴾

"The observer is one who reflects on what he has heard, reflects upon what he has seen, and makes use of his instructive experience in choosing to tread on clear paths wherein he can avoid falling into hallows and staying into pitfalls."[108]

There is a statement narrated from Imam al-Sādiq (AS):

﴿زعمت ان الاشياء لاتدرك الا باالحواس فانّي اخبرك انّه ليس للحواس دلالة علي الاشياء و لافيها معرفة الا بالقلب فانه دليلها و معرفها الاشياء التي تدّعي ان القلب لايعرفها الا بها ... ان القلب يفكر بالعقل الذي فيه ... انّ الله تعالي جعل القلب مدبّرا للجسد، به يسمع و به يبصر و هو القاضي والامير عليه، و به ينزل الفرح و الحزن، و به ينزل الالم، ان فسد شيئ من الحواس بقي علي حاله، وان فسد القلب ذهب جميعا حتي لايسمع و لايبصر﴾

"You thought things could not be felt except through senses. Let me advise you that senses do not directly lead you to objects, and we know objects only through the channel of heart; therefore, it is heart which directs the senses and presents objects to the senses, the objects that you (mistakenly) claim are not known to the heart but through senses ... Heart reflects by the intellect which it possesses. The Almighty God made heart the administrator of the body and it hears and sees through the heart. Heart is the judge and ruler of the body. Should heart delay, the body cannot proceed, should it proceed the body cannot tarry. Senses see and hear through the heart; should it order senses, they obey; should it hinder them, they stop. Happiness and sorrow, too, befall man through the heart and make him endure them. If senses fail and decay, heart goes on functioning; but with the decay of heart all the senses disappear- man neither sees nor hears." [109]

3. The Qur'anic verses indicate that in addition to sense-rooted

cognitions, there are non-sensory cognitions, too. These verses fall into two groups:

a) In one group of the verses Allah refutes the arguments of the people who consider their external senses as the only reliable source for their knowledge:

﴿واذا قلتم يا موسي لن نؤمن لك حتي نري الله جهرةً فاخذتكم الصاعقة و انتم تنظرون﴾ (البقرة/ 55)

"And when you said: O Mūsā! We will not believe in you until we see Allah manifestly, so the punishment overtook you while you looked on."

(Sūrah 2: 55)

﴿وقالوا لن نؤمن لك حتي تفجرلنا من الارض ينبوعاً او تكون لك جنة من نخيل و عنب فتفجر الانهار خلالها تفجيراً او تسقط السماء كما زعمت علينا كسفاً او تأتي بالله والملائكة قبيلا او يكون لك بيت من زخرف او ترقي في السماء ولن نؤمن لرقيّك حتّي تنزّل علينا كتاباً نقروه قل سبحان ربي هل كنت الّا بشراً رسولاً﴾ (الاسراء/ 93-90)

"And they said: 'We will by no means believe in you until you cause a fountain to gush forth form the earth for us.'

'Or you should have a garden of palms and grapes in the midst of which you should cause rivers to flow forth gushing out.'

'Or you should cause the heaven to come down up on us in pieces as you think, or bring Allah and the angels face to face (with us)'

'Or you should have a house of gold, or you should ascend into heaven, and we will not believe in your ascending until you bring down to us a book which we may read.' Say: 'Glory be to my Lord. I am not but a mortal messenger?'"

(Sūrah 17: 90-93)

﴿يعلمون ظاهراً من الحيوة الدنيا و هم عن الآخرة هم غافلون﴾ (الروم/ 7)

"They know the outward of this world's life, but of the Hereafter they are absolutely heedless."

(Sūrah 30: 7)

b) The Qur'an repeatedly reminds us that we do not perceive many of the realities of the physical world through external senses:

﴿الله الذي رفع السموات بغير عمد ترونها ...﴾ (الرعد/ 2)

"Allah is He who raised the heavens without any pillars you see..."

(Sūrah 13: 2)

﴿فلا اقسم بما تبصرون و ما لاتبصرون﴾ (الحاقة/ 39-38)

"But nay! I swear by that which you see, and that which you see not."

(Sūrah 69: 38-39)

﴿سبحان الذي خلق الازواج كلها مما تنبت الارض و من انفسهم و مما لايعلمون﴾ (يس/ 36)

"Glory be to Him who created pairs of all things, of what the earth grow, and of their kind and of what they do not know."

(Sūrah 36: 36)

We also learn from the Qur'an that only Allah is aware of the mysteries in the heavens and the earth, and those to whom Allah has granted this bliss:

﴿و لله غيب السموات والارض و اليه يرجع الامر كله﴾ (هود/ 123)

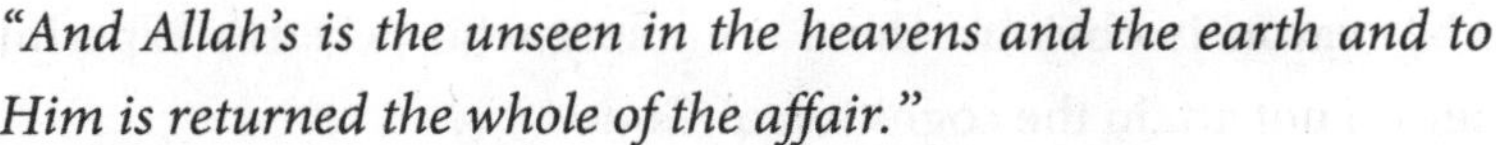

"And Allah's is the unseen in the heavens and the earth and to Him is returned the whole of the affair."

(Sūrah 11: 123)

﴿قل الله اعلم بما لبثوا له غيب السموات والارض ...﴾ (الكهف/ 26)

"Say; Allah knows best how long they remained: To Him are (known) the unseen things of the heavens and the earth ..."

(Sūrah 18: 26)

﴿عالم الغيب فلا يظهر علي غيبه احداً الا من ارتضي من رسول ...﴾

(الجن/ 26-27)

"The knower of the unseen. So He does not reveal His secrets to any except to him who He regards as a messenger."

(Sūrah 72: 26-27)

> Unfortunately, in recent centuries, some Muslim scholars have wrongly propounded the view that experiments are the only means of acquiring knowledge, and that the experimental study of the book of nature suffices to know God.[110]

We, too, agree that experimentation and observation are indispensable tools for understanding nature. We even believe that the Muslims' work in this field has been quite inadequate. But we also believe that our understanding of nature is not purely a matter of the senses. Besides, our observations and experiments cannot be the source of any knowledge unless they are channelized via intellectual principles.

In the matter of scientific cognition of God, we are of the same opinion as that expressed by the late scholar Murtadā Mutahharī:

"The boundary of experiment is only the cognition of the works of God, but the cognition of God through the works known by experiment is a kind of pure intellectual deduction."[111]

The reason is obvious: there are many who perform experiments, but they do not attain the cognition of God.

Science only nominally consists of issues verifiable by experimental methods. But, many issues have not directly resulted from experiment. In fact, one may say that in all natural sciences, our knowledge is mainly based on deduction, and we have not obtained any of the rules and laws in physics or chemistry from experiment, but they are based on intellectual deductions. The matter itself has come to be known through intellectual deduction, because experiments in physics or chemistry provide us only with the properties of matter.

This view, that most of our knowledge of the physical world has come through intellectual deduction, is not shared by most scholars in natural sciences in recent years. But as Albert Einstein[112] rightly advised, we had better not listen to what physicists say, but rather see what they do. The fact is that many of the scientists with positivistic views, have overlooked their own claim. Moreover, among western scholars in natural sciences, we find some outstanding figures who admit the decisive role of intellectual deductions and interpretation in our knowledge of natural phenomena. As Max Planck put it:

> *"The ideal aim before the mind of the physicist is to understand the external world of reality. But the means which he uses to attain this end are what are known in physical science as 'measurements', and these give no direct information about external reality. They are only a register or representation of reactions to physical phenomena. As such they contain no explicit information and have to be interpreted. As Helmhotlz said, measurements furnish the physicist with a sign which he must interpret, just as a language expert interprets the text of some prehistoric document that belongs to a culture utterly unknown. The first thing which the language expert assumes – and must assume if his work is to have any practical meaning –*

is that the document in question contains some reasonable message which has been stated according to some system of grammatical rules or symbols. In the same way the physicist must assume that the physical universe is governed by some system of laws which can be understood, even though he cannot hold out himself the prospect of being able to understand them in a comprehensive way or to discover their character and manner of operation with anything like a full degree of certitude.

Taking it, then, that the external world of reality is governed by a system of laws, the physicist now constructs a synthesis of concepts and theorems; and this synthesis is called the scientific picture of the physical universe. It is a representation of the real world itself in so far as it corresponds as closely as possible to the information which the research measurements have supplied. Once he has accomplished this, the researcher can assert, without having to fear the contradiction of facts, that he has discovered one side of the outer world of reality, though of course he can never logically demonstrate the truth of the assertion." [113]

In a lecture, delivered by Einstein at Oxford University in 1933, under the title of "*On Methods of Theoretical Physics*", he said:

"... Newton, the first creator of a comprehensive, workable system of theoretical physics, still believed that the basic concepts and laws of his system could be derived from experience. This is no doubt the meaning of his saying, 'hypotheses non fingo'.

Actually the concepts of time and space appeared at that time to present no difficulties. The concepts of mass, inertia, and force, and the laws connecting them, seemed to be drawn directly from experience. Once this basis is accepted, the expression for the force of gravitation appears derivable from experience, and it was reasonable to expect the same in regard to other forces.

We can indeed see from Newton's formulation of it that the concept of absolute space, which comprised that of absolute rest, made him feel uncomfortable; he realized that there seemed to be nothing in experience corresponding to this last concept. He was also not quite comfortable about the introduction of forces operating at a distance. But the tremendous partial success of his doctrines may well have prevented him and the physicists of the eighteenth and nineteenth centuries from recognizing the fictitious character of the foundations of his system.

The natural philosophers of those days were, on the contrary, most of them possessed with the idea that fundamental concepts and postulates of physics were not in the logical sense, free inventions of the human mind, but could be deduced from experience by 'abstraction' that is to say, by logical means. A clear recognition of the erroneousness of this notion really came with the general theory of relativity, which showed that one could take account of wider range of empirical facts, and that, too, in a more satisfactory and complete manner, on a foundation quite different from the Newtonian. But quite apart from the question of the superiority of one or the other, the fictitious character of fundamental principles is perfectly evident from the fact that we can point to two essentially different principles, both of which correspond with experience to a large extent; this proves at the same time that every attempt at a logical deduction of the basic concepts and postulates of mechanics from elementary experiences is doomed to failure.

If, then, it is true that the axiomatic basis of theoretical physics cannot be extracted from experience but must be freely invented, can we ever hope to find the right way? Nay, more, has this right way any existence outside our illusions? Can we hope to be guided safely by experience at all when there exist theories (such as classical mechanics) which to a large extent do justice to experience, without getting to the root of the matter? I answer without hesitation that there is, in my opinion, a right way, and that we are capable of finding it. Our experience hitherto justifies us in believing that nature is the realization of the simplest conceivable mathematical ideas. I am convinced that we can discover by means of purely mathematical constructions, the concepts and the laws connecting them with each other, which furnish the key to the understanding of natural phenomena. Experience may suggest the appropriate mathematical concepts, but they most certainly cannot be deduced from it. Experience remains, of course, the sole criterion of the physical utility of a mathematical construction. But the creative principle resides in mathematics. In a certain sense, therefore, I hold it true that pure thought can grasp reality, as the ancients dreamed."[114]

In his book *Physics and Beyond*, Heisenberg writes[115] that in the year 1926 he was of the opinion that Einstein still believed in the positivistic view of Mach, that is, he believed that only observable quantities should be included in physical theories. Therefore, when Einstein said: 'but you do not seriously believe that none but observable magnitudes must go into a physical theory?', Heisenberg asked with some surprise: "Isn't that precisely what you have done with relativity? ... After all, you did stress the fact that it is impermissible to speak of absolute time, simply because absolute time cannot be observed; that only clock readings, be it in the moving reference system or the system at rest, are relevant to the determination of time." Einstein, then, admitted:

"Possibly I did use this kind of reasoning but it is nonsense all the same. Perhaps I could put it more diplomatically by saying that it may be heuristically useful to keep in mind what one has actually observed. But in principle, it is quite wrong to try founding a theory on observable magnitudes alone. In reality the

very opposite happens. It is the theory which decides what we can observe."

Philip Frank in his biography of Einstein says[116] that he once told Einstein that he himself had introduced the positivistic view into physics. Einstein answered: "A good joke should not be repeated too often".

Our purpose in citing these quotations is to point out that many of the recent outstanding research scholars, too, have been fully aware of the inadequacy of experiments for the interpretation of nature. Otherwise, we do not doubt the importance and indispensibity of experiments, and Muslim researchers should not forget the message carried in such verses:

﴿قل سيروا في الارض فانظروا كيف بدأ الخلق ...﴾ (العنكبوت/ 20)

"Say: Travel in the earth and see how He made the first creation ..."

(Sūrah 29: 20)

﴿قل انظروا ما ذا في السموات والارض ...﴾ (يونس/ 101)

"Say: Consider what is it that is in the heavens and the earth ..."

(Sūrah 10: 101)

We should also bear in mind that while the Qur'an invites us to the experimental study of nature, it also points out the importance of reasoning, and teaches us not to be satisfied with mere sensory experience; rather, by observing what is beyond the observable part of nature, we may move closer to the Creator of nature.

2. The role of revelation and inspiration in understanding nature

It is deduced from some verses in the Qur'an that the true teacher of all sciences is the Omniscient God:

﴿اقرأ باسم ربك الذي خلق... الذي علم بالقلم علم الانسان ما لم يعلم﴾
(العلق/ 5-1)

"Read in the name of your Lord Who created... Who taught (to write) with the pen. Taught man what he knew not."

(Sūrah 96: 1-5)

﴿خلق الانسان علمه البيان﴾ (الرحمن/ 4-3)

"He created man, and taught him to talk."

(Sūrah 55: 3-4)

﴿و علم آدم الاسماء كلها ...﴾ (البقرة/ 31)

"And taught Adam all the Names, ..."

(Sūrah 2: 31)

The least we can infer from these verses is that God has endowed man with the talent to acquire knowledge and has given him the necessary means. But some Muslim philosophers believe that the role of observations in the perception of a priori knowledge and the role of preliminary matters in the perception of theoretical subjects is to prepare man's soul to fully benefit from the spiritual world.[117]

In fact, the main source of inspiration in the matter of knowledge for human beings is the Omniscient Donor of knowledge, Allah. But the extent of relation between human beings and this Source differs from person to person. Some think and get nowhere, whereas some others find some truth through meditation; and yet there are some others who become aware of many realities with only little speculation.

Some Qur'anic verses indicate that besides ordinary channels of observation, meditation and intellection, there is a more direct way of attaining the knowledge of the realities of the world through the Donor of knowledge; but this way is not a general one and only a handful of selected believers have access to it. These verses may be divided into several groups.

1. It is stated in some verses that God reveals special knowledge to certain select believers:

﴿و قتل داود جالوت و آتاه الله الملك والحكمة و علمه ممّا يشاء ...﴾ (البقرة/ 251)

"And Dāwūd (David) slew Jālūt, and God gave him kingdom and wisdom, and taught him of what he pleased ..."

(Sūrah 2: 251)

﴿ربّ قد آتيتني من الملك و علمتني من تأويل الاحاديث ...﴾ (يوسف/ 101)

"My Lord. Thou hast given me of the kingdom and taught me of the interpretation of sayings ..."

(Sūrah 12: 101)

﴿فوجد عبداً من عبادنا آتيناه رحمة من عندنا و علمناه من لدنّا علماً﴾ (الكهف/ 65)

"Then they found one from among Our servants whom We had granted from Us and whom We had taught knowledge from Ourselves."

(Sūrah 18: 65)

﴿... اذ قال الله يا عيسي ابن مريم اذكر نعمتي عليك و علي والدتك... واذ علمتك الكتاب و الحكمة والتورية والانجيل ...﴾ (المائدة/ 110)

"...When God will say: o' 'Īsā (Jesus Christ) son of Maryam (Mary), remember My favour on you and on your mother ... and when I taught you the Book and the Wisdom and the Tawrāh (Torah) and the Injīl (Bible) ..."

(Sūrah 5: 110)

﴿... و انّه لذو علم لما علّمناه ولكن اكثر الناس لايعلمون﴾ (يوسف/ 68)

"And surely he was possessed of knowledge because We had given him knowledge, but most people do not know."

(Sūrah 12: 68)

﴿و داود و سليمان اذ يحكمان في الحرث ... ففهّمناها سليمان وكلاً اتينا حكماً و سخّرنا مع داود الجبال يسبّحن والطير و كنّا فاعلين و علّمناه صنعة لبوس لكم لتحصنكم من بأسكم فهل انتم شاكرون﴾ (الأنبياء / 80-78)

"And Dāwūd (David) and Sulaymān (Solomon) when they gave judgement concerning the field when the people's sheep pastured therein by night, and we were bearer of witness to their judgement. So we made Sulaymān to understand; and to each one We gave wisdom and knowledge; and We made the mountains, and the birds to celebrate Our praise with Dāwūd; and We were the doers. And We taught him the making of coats of mail for you, that they might protect you in your wars; will you then be grateful?"

(Sūrah 21: 78-80)

In some of the verses, the idea that this way of teaching can be accomplished through human teachers has been rejected:

﴿ان هو الّا وحي يوحي **علّمه** شديد القوي﴾ (النجم/ 4-5)

"It is naught but revelation that is revealed. The Lord of Mighty Power has taught him."

(Sūrah 53: 4-5)

﴿و لقد نعلم انّهم يقولون انّما **يعلّمه** بشر ...﴾ (النحل/ 103)

"And certainly We know that they say: only a mortal teaches him."

(Sūrah 16: 103)

﴿... و انزل الله عليك الكتاب والحكمة و علّمك ما لم تكن تعلم ...﴾
(النساء/ 113)

"And God has revealed to you the Book and the wisdom, and He has taught you what you did not know."

(Sūrah 4: 113)

2. Another group of verses indicate revelation to prophets:

﴿ذلك ممّا اوحي اليك ربك من الحكمة ...﴾ (الاسراء/ 39)

"This is of what your Lord has revealed to you of wisdom ..."

(Sūrah 17: 39)

﴿فاوحي الى عبده ما اوحي ما كذب الفؤاد ما رأي﴾ (النجم/ 11-10)

"And He revealed to His servant what He revealed. His heart lies not of what he saw."

(Sūrah 53: 10-11)

﴿انّا اوحينا اليك كما اوحينا الى نوح والنبيين من بعده و اوحينا الى ابراهيم و اسمعيل و اسحق و يعقوب والاسباط و عيسي و ايوب و يونس و هرون و سليمان و آتينا داود زبورا﴾ (النساء/ 163)

"Surely We have revealed to you as We revealed to Nūh (Noah), and the prophets after him, and We revealed to Ibrāhīm (Abraham) and Ismāīl (Ismael) and Ishāq (Isaac) and Yaqūb (Jacob) and the tribes and 'Īsā (Jesus Christ) and Ayyūb (Job) and Yūnus (Jonah) and Hārūn (Aaron) and Sulaymān (Solomon) and We gave to Dāwūd (David) Psalms"

(Sūrah 4: 163)

﴿و اوحينا الى موسي ان الق عصاك فاذا هي تلقف ما يأفكون﴾ (الاعراف/ 117)

"And We revealed to Mūsā (Moses) saying: Cast your rod, then, lo! It devoured the lies they told."

(Sūrah 7: 117)

﴿اكان للناس عجباً ان اوحينا الي رجل منهم ان انذر الناس ...﴾ (يونس/ 2)

"What! Is it a wonder to the people We revealed to a man from among themselves saying: 'Warn the people'...?"

(Sūrah 10: 2)

﴿و اوحينا الى موسىٰ و اخيه تبوّا لقومكما بمصر بيوتاً ...﴾ (يونس/ 87)

"And We revealed to Mūsā and his brother, saying: Take for your people houses to abide in..."

(Sūrah 10: 87)

﴿فاوحينا اليه ان اصنع الفلك ...﴾ (المؤمنون/ 27)

"So We revealed to him saying: 'Make the Ark'..."

(Sūrah 23: 27)

﴿ذلك من انباء الغيب نوحيه اليك ...﴾ (آل‌عمران/ 44)

"This is of the announcements relating to the unseen which We reveal to you."

(Sūrah 3: 44)

﴿و ما ارسلنا من قبلك الّا رجالاً نوحي اليهم ...﴾ (النحل/ 43)

"And We did not send before you any but men to whom We sent revelation ..."

(Sūrah 16: 43)

﴿قل انّما انا بشر مثلكم يوحي اليَّ ...﴾ (الكهف/ 110)

"Say: I am only a mortal like you, it is Revealed to me..."

(Sūrah 18: 110)

3. Yet another group of verses indicate the possibility of revelation for people other than prophets:

﴿و اذ اوحيت الى الحواريين ان امنوا بي و برسولي قالوا امنّا و اشهد باننا مسلمون﴾ (المائده/ 111)

"And when I revealed to the disciples, saying, Believe in Me and My messenger, they said: we believe and bear witness that we submit (ourselves),"

(Sūrah 5: 111)

﴿و اوحينا الى ام موسي ان ارضعيه ...﴾ (القصص/ 7)

"And we revealed to Mūsā's mother, saying: Give him suck ..."

(Sūrah 28: 7)

In this case, "revelation" is interpreted[118] as "inspiration". Of course, revelation has been used in other senses as well.[119]

What we may conclude from these verses is the possibility of learning from the Donor of knowledge through a channel different from the common channel of observation and thinking. This, too, has different levels: the highest level of revelation is reserved for prophets only, and according to the glorious verse:

﴿و ما كان لبشران بكلمه الله الا وحياً أومن وراء حجاب او يرسل رسولاً فيوحي باذنه مايشاء ... ﴾ (الشوري/ 51)

"And it is not for any mortal that God should speak to him except by revelation or from behind a veil, or by sending a messenger and revealing by His permission what He pleases ..."

(Sūrah 42: 51)

it is done through a direct inducement of the meaning in the prophet's heart, or by the creation of words or by sending an angel messenger to him.[120] At the lower levels, this is done through inspiration, which is variously termed as *kashf* [كشف] or *'ilhām* (الهام).

Muslim philosophers believed that the people having talent for attaining such immediate knowledge are those who are endowed with a saintly faculty (قوة قدسية). To explain their reasoning we take a look back, and notice that one of the channels to cognition is (logical) thinking. In thinking, the mind undergoes a two-stage movement, and shuttles between the known and the unknown. In thinking one seeks a middle term that is common in both the given propositions with the help of which he hopes to understand the unknown. In general, finding the middle term requires certain premises. Yet in certain special cases some people may reach the middle term and the conclusion without forming a syllogism in their minds.[121] This mental talent which takes one to the goal without following logical steps is called 'intuition' (حدس) and in its highest form has been called 'the saintly faculty' (قوة قدسيه). A person having this gift can know many realities the use of his sensory and rational faculties. Ibn Sina (Avicenna) in his *al-Ishārāt* says[122] that the following Qur'anic phrase refers to this special mental faculty:

﴿يكاد زيتها يضيء و لولم تمسسه نار﴾ (النور/ 35)

"The oil where of almost gives light though fire touch it not ..."

(Sūrah 24:35)

and he confirms its existence in the following statement:

"You may wish to have more evidence to prove the existence of the saintly faculty gift. So hark! Do you not know that 'intuition' exists, and people possess different levels of reflection. Some are so dull and stupid that they find no way to their goal; some others are moderately intelligent and can make use of their reasoning power and some others, more intelligent, can perceive intelligibles through intuition. This intelligence differs from person to person; at the lowest level, man is completely deprived from intuition; at the highest level, one does not need to learn (through regular course) or think through logical categories (for knowing the reality)." [123]

Now we are in a position to say that in the same way that revelation has various degrees, as asserted in the following verse:

﴿تلك الرسل فضّلنا بعضهم علي بعض منهم من كلّم الله و رفع بعضهم درجات و اتينا عيسي ابن مريم البينات و ايّدناه بروح القدس ...﴾ (البقرة/ 253)

"We have made some of these messengers to excel the others; among them are they to whom God spoke, and some of them He exalted by (many) degrees of rank; We gave clear miracles to 'Īsā (Jesus) son of Maryam (Mary), and strengthened him with the Holy Spirit."

(Sūrah 2: 253),

Inspiration, too, has different levels – though on the whole it is lower than revelation. Some people enjoy this gift at its highest level and others possess it in its weaker forms. For the former, realities are made manifest without the effort of reflection, while the latter attain new knowledge through their own endeavours.

Some of the contemporary scholars have accepted the presence of this ability in some people. As Dr. Alexis Carrel put it:

"Obviously, great discoveries are not the product of intelligence alone. Men of genius, in addition to their powers of observation and comprehension, posses other qualities, such as intuition and creative imagination. Through intuition they learn things ignored by other men, they perceive relations between seemingly isolated phenomena. They unconsciously feel the presence of the unknown treasure. All great men are endowed with intuition. They know, without analysis, without reasoning, what is important for them to know. A true leader of men does not need psychological tests, or reference cards, when choosing his subordinates. A good judge, without going into the details of legal arguments, and even, according to Cardozo, starting from erroneous premises is capable of rendering a just sentence. A great scientist instinctively takes the path leading to a discovery. This phenomenon, in former times, was called inspiration.

Men of science belong to two different types - the logical and the intuitive. Science owes its progress to both forms of mind. Mathematics, although a purely logical structure, nevertheless makes use of intuition. Among the mathematicians there are intuitives and logicians, analysts and geometricians. Hermite and Weierstrass were intuitives, Riemann and Bertrand, logicians. The discoveries of intuition have always to be developed by logic. In ordinary life, as in science, intuition is a powerful but dangerous means of acquiring knowledge. Sometimes it can hardly be distinguished from illusion. Those who rely upon it entirely are liable to mistakes. It is far from being always trustworthy. But the great man, or the simple whose heart is pure, can be led by it to the summits of mental and spiritual life. It is a strange quality. To apprehend reality without the help of intelligence appears inexplicable. One of the aspects of intuition resembles a very rapid deduction from an instantaneous observation. The Knowledge that great physicians sometimes possess concerning the present and the future state of their patients is of such a nature. A similar phenomenon occurs when one appraises in a flash a man's value, or senses his virtues and his vices. But under another aspect, intuition takes place quite independently of observation and reasoning. We may be led by it to our goal when we do not how to attain this goal and even where it is located. This mode of knowledge is closely analogous to clairvoyance, to the sixth sense of Charles Richet."[124]

And in the words of the Nobel laureate physicist Charles H. Townes:

"Religion's discoveries often come by great revelations. Scientific knowledge, in the popular mind, comes by logical deduction, or by the accumulation of data which is analyzed by established methods in order to draw generalizations called laws. But such a description of scientific discovery is a travesty on the real thing. Most of the important scientific discoveries come about very differently and are much more closely akin to revelation. The term itself is generally not used for scientific discovery, since we are in the habit of reserving revelation for the religious realm. In scientific circles one speaks of intuition, accidental discovery, or says simply that "he had a wonderful idea."

If we compare how great scientific ideas arrive, they look remarkably like religious revelation viewed in a non-mystical way. Think of Moses in the desert, long troubled and wondering about the problem of saving the children of Israel, when suddenly he had a revelation by the burning bush. A similar pattern is seen in many of the revelations of the Old and New Testaments. Think of Gautama the Buddha who traveled and inquired for years in an effort to understand what was good, and then one day sat down quietly under a Bo tree where his ideas were revealed. Similarly, the scientist, after hard work and much emotional and intellectual commitment to a troubling problem, sometimes suddenly sees the answer. Such ideas much more often come during off-moments than while confronting data. A striking and well-known example is the discovery of the benzene ring by Kekulé, who while musing at his fireside was led to the idea by the vision of a snakelike molecule taking its tail in its mouth. We cannot yet describe the human process which leads to the creation of an important and substantially new scientific. But it is clear that the great scientific discoveries, the real leaps, do not usually come from the so-called "scientific method", but rather more as did Kekulé's – with perhaps less picturesque imagery, but by revelations which are just as real." [125]

Finally I would like to mention that though inspiration and enlightenment are means to attain knowledge, not everybody receives this gift:

﴿ذلك فضل الله يؤتيه من يشاء ...﴾ (الجمعه/ 4)

"That is God's grace; He grants it to whom He pleases."

(Sūrah 62: 4)

The only way which is open to everyone is the channel of observation and reflection while aiming at attaining the knowledge of nature. The conditions leading to proper result shall be discussed in a later part of our discourse.

Stages in Understanding Nature

We have already seen that from the viewpoint of Qur'an man has the capacity to understand nature.

With the use of external senses and intellect, human beings should get closer to God through understanding Divine signs. Here we have to mention that wherever there is a reference in the Qur'an to the Divine evidences in the physical world, Allah attributes the ability of understanding them to special groups of people. Here are a few examples:

On meditators:

﴿هو الذي انزل من السماء ماءً لكم منه شراب و منه شجر فيه تسيمون ينبت لكم به الزرع والزيتون والنخيل والاعناب و من كل الثمرات ان في ذلك لاية لقوم يتفكرون﴾ (النحل/ 11-10)

"He it is who sends down water from the cloud for you, it gives drink and by it (grow) the trees upon which you pasture. He causes to grow for you thereby herbage, and the olive, and the palm tree, and the grapes, and of all the fruits, most surely there is a sign in this for a people who reflect."

(Sūrah 16: 10-11)

﴿و سخّر لكم ما في السموات و ما في الارض جميعاً منه. انّ في ذلك لايات لقوم يتفكرون﴾ (الجاثيه/ 13)

"And He has made subservient to you whatsoever is in the heavens and whatsoever is in the earth, all, from himself; most surely there are signs in this for a people who reflect."

(Sūrah 45: 13)

On the wise:

﴿انّ في خلق السموات والارض و اختلاف الليل والنهار و الفلك التي تجري في البحر بما ينفع الناس و ما انزل الله من السماء من ماء فاحيا به الارض بعد موتها و بثّ فيها من كلّ دابّة و تصريف الرياح والسحاب المسخر بين السماء والارض لايات لقوم يعقلون﴾ (البقرة/ 164)

"Most surely in the creation of the heavens and the earth, The alternation of the night and the day, and the ships that run in the sea with that which profits men, and the water that Allah sends down from the cloud, then gives life with it to the earth after its death and spreads in it all (kinds of) animals, and the changing of the winds and the clouds made subservient between the heaven and the earth, there are signs for a people who ponder."

(Sūrah 2: 164)

﴿و سخّر لكم الليل والنهار والشمس والقمر والنجوم مسخّرات بامره انّ في ذلك لآيات لقوم يعقلون﴾ (النحل/ 12)

"And He has made subservient for you the night and the day and the sun and the moon, and the stars are made subservient by His commandment; most surely there are signs in this for a people who ponder."

(Sūrah 16: 12)

On the people who understand:

﴿انّ في خلق السموات والارض و اختلاف الليل والنهار لآيات لاولي الالباب﴾ (آل‌عمران/ 190)

"Most surely in the creation of the heavens and the earth and the alternation of the night and the day there are signs for men who understand."

(Sūrah 3: 190)

﴿الم تر انّ الله انزل من السماء ماءً فسلكه ينابيع في الارض ثم يخرج به زرعاً مختلفاً الوانه ثم يهيج فتريه مصفراً ثم يجعله حطاماً انّ في ذلك لذكري لاولي الالباب﴾ (الزمر/ 21)

"Do you not see that Allah sends down water from the cloud, then makes it go along in the earth in springs, then brings forth therewith herbage of various colours, then it withers so that you see it becoming yellow, then makes it a thing crushed and broken into pieces? Most surely there is a reminder in this for the men of understanding."

(Sūrah 39: 21)

On the believers:

﴿انّ في السموات والارض لآيات للمؤمنين﴾ (الجاثية/ 3)

"Most surely in the heavens and the earth there are some signs for the believers."

(Sūrah 45: 3)

﴿الم يروا انّا جعلنا الليل ليسكنوا فيه والنهار مبصراً انّ في ذلك لآيات لقوم يؤمنون﴾ (النمل/ 86)

"Do they not consider that We have made the night that they may rest therein, and the day to give light? Most surely there are signs in this for a people who believe."

(Sūrah 27: 86)

On the pious:

﴿انّ في اختلاف الليل والنهار و ما خلق الله في السموات والارض لآيات لقوم يتّقون﴾ (يونس/ 6)

"Most surely in the variation of the night and the day, and what Allah has created in the heavens and the earth, there are signs for a people who guard (against) evil."

(Sūrah 10: 6)

﴿خذوا ما آتيناكم بقوّة واذكروا ما فيه لعلكم تتقون﴾ (البقرة/ 63)

"Take hold of the law we have given you with firmness and bear in mind what is in it, so that you may guard (against) evil."

(Sūrah 2: 63)

On the learned:

﴿و من آياته خلق السموات والارض و اختلاف السنتكم و الوانكم انّ في ذلك لآيات للعالمين﴾ (الروم/ 22)

"And one of His signs is the creation of the heavens and the earth and the diversity of your tongues and colours; most surely there are signs in this for the learned."

(Sūrah 30: 22)

﴿هوالذي جعل الشمس ضياء والقمر نوراً و قدّره منازل لتعلموا عدد السنين والحساب ما خلق الله ذلك الّا بالحق، يفصّل الآيات لقوم يعلمون﴾ (يونس/ 5)

"He it is who made the sun a shining brightness and the moon a light, and ordained for mansions that you might know the computation of years and the reckoning. Allah did not create it

but in truth; He makes the signs manifest for a people who know."

(Sūrah 10: 5)

On the mindful:

﴿ما ذرأ لكم في الارض مختلفاً الوانه انّ في ذلك لآية لقوم يذّكرون﴾
(النحل/ 13)

"And what he has created in the earth of varied hues; most surely there is a sign in this for a people who are mindful."

(Sūrah 16: 13)

﴿و من كل شيئ خلقنا زوجين لعلّكم تذكرون﴾ (الذاريات/ 49)

"And of everything we have created a pair that you may be mindful."

(Sūrah 51: 49)

On those who listen to truth:

﴿و من آياته منامكم بالليل والنهار و ابتغاؤكم من فضله انّ في ذلك لآيات لقوم يسمعون﴾ (الروم/ 23)

"And one of His signs is your sleeping and your seeking of His grace by night and (by) day; most surely there are signs in this for a people who would hear."

(Sūrah 30: 23)

﴿والله انزل من السماء ماءً فاحيا به الارض بعد موتها انّ في ذلك لآية لقوم يسمعون﴾ (النحل/ 65)

"And Allah has sent down water from the cloud and there with given life to the earth after its death; most surely there is a sign in this for a people who would listen."

(Sūrah 16: 65)

On the people who are sure:

﴿و في خلقكم وما يبثّ من دابّة آيات لقوم يوقنون﴾ (الجاثيه/ 4)

"And in your (own) creation and in what He spreads abroad of animals there are signs for a people that are sure."

(Sūrah 45: 4)

﴿و في الارض آيات للموقنين و في انفسكم افلا تبصرون﴾ (الذاريات/ 21-20)

"And in the earth there are signs for those who are sure; And in your own soul (too); will you not then see?"

(Sūrah 51: 20-21)

On those who examine truth, have insight, and understand:

﴿و هوالذي أنشأكم من نفس واحدة فمستقر و مستودع قد فصّلنا الآيات لقوم يفقهون﴾ (الانعام/ 98)

"And He is who has brought you into being from a single soul, then there is (for you) a resting place and a depository; indeed we have made plain the signs for a people who understand."

(Sūrah 6: 98)

﴿فاخذتهم الصيحة مشرقين فجعلنا عاليها سافلها و امطرنا عليهم حجارة من سجّيل انّ في ذلك لآيات للمتوسلين﴾ (الحجر/ 75-73)

"So the rumbling overtook them (while) entering upon the time of sunrise. Thus did we turn it upside down, and rained down upon them stones of what has been decreed. Surely in this are signs for those who examine."

(Sūrah 15: 73-75)

﴿كلوا و ارعوا أنعامكم انّ في ذلك لآيات لاولي النهي﴾ (طه/ 54)

"Eat and pasture you cattle; most surely there are signs in this for those endowed with understanding."

(Sūrah 20: 54)

What we understand from the words: *tafakkur*, *taaqqul*, *tafaqquh*, etc. used in the Qur'an is that they refer to different degrees of intellectual perception and some degrees are indispensable for some other degrees. For example, by comparing the following verses:

﴿انّ في خلق السموات والارض و اختلاف الليل والنهار لآيات لاولي الالبابِ الذين يذكرون الله قياما و قعودا و علي جنوبهم و يتفكرون في خلق السموات والارض ربنا ما خلقت هذا باطلا ...﴾ (آل‌عمران/ 191-190)

"Most surely in the creation of the heavens and the earth and the alternation of the night and the day there are signs for men who understand. Those who remember Allah standing and sitting and being on their sides and reflect on the creation of the heavens and the earth: our Lord! You have not created this in vain. Glory be to You; save us then from the chastisement of the fire!"

(Sūrah 3: 190-191)

﴿انّ في خلق السموات والارض و اختلاف الليل والنهار ... لآيات لقوم يعقلون﴾ (البقرة/ 164)

"Most surly in the creation of the heavens and the earth and the alternation of the night and the day...there are signs for a people who understand."

(Sūrah 2: 164)

﴿انّ في اختلاف الليل والنهار و ما خلق الله في السموات والارض لآيات لقوم يتقون﴾ (يونس/ 6)

"Most surely in the alternation of the night and the day, and what Allah has created in the heavens and earth, there are signs for a people who guard (against evil)."

(Sūrah 10: 6)

﴿... و تزودوا فانّ خيرالزاد التقوي واتقون يا اولي الالباب﴾ (البقرة/ 197)

..." and make provision, for surely the provision is the guarding of oneself, and be careful (of your duty) to Me, O men of understanding."

(Sūrah 2: 197)

﴿و تلك الامثال نضربها للناس و ما يعقلها الا العالمون﴾ (العنكبوت/ 43)

"And (as for) these examples, We set them forth for the people and none understand them but the learned."

(Sūrah 29: 43)

It may be concluded that *'Ulel-Albāb* (possessors of "reasoning faculty" have meditation, piety and knowledge. Their other characteristics are: listening and hearing the right word, avoiding the fallacies or illusions, worshipping God, having wisdom, being mindful and taking an example of the past experiences (of ancestors). These characteristics are deducible from the following verses:

﴿... فبشر عباد الذين يستمعون القول فيتبعون احسنه اولئك الذين هديٰهم الله و اولئك هم اولوالالباب﴾ (الزمر/ 18-17)

"Say give good news to My servants who listen to the word, then follow the best of it; those are they whom Allah has guided, and it is they who are the men of understanding."

(Sūrah 39: 17-18)

﴿هوالذي انزل عليك الكتاب منه آيات محكمات هن أمالكتاب و آخر متشابهات فامّا الذين في قلوبهم زيغ فيتبّعون ما تشابه منه ابتغاء تأويله و ما يعلم تأويله الّا الله والراسخون في العلم يقولون آمنّا به كل من عند ربّنا و ما يذكر الّا اولـوالالبـاب﴾ (آلعمران/ 7)

"He it is who has revealed the book to you; some of its verses are decisive, they are the basis of the Book, and others are allegorical; then as for those in whose hearts there is perversity, they follow the part of it which is all allegorical, seeking to mislead, and seeking to give it (their own) interpretation, but none knows its interpretation except Allah, and those who are firmly rooted in knowledge, who say: we believe in it, it is all from our Lord; and none do mind except those having understanding."

(Sūrah 3: 7)

﴿أمّن هو قانت أناء الليل ساجداً و قائماً يحذرالآخرة و يرجوا رحمة ربّه قل هل يستوي الذين يعلمون والذين لا يعلمون انّما يتذكر اولواالالباب﴾ (الزمر/ 9)

"What! He who is obedient during hours of the night prostrating himself and standing, takes care of the Hereafter and hopes for the mercy of his Lord! Say: 'Are those who know and those who do not know alike?' Only the men of understanding are mindful."

(Sūrah 39:9)

﴿يؤتي الحكمة من يشاء و من يؤت الحكمة فقد اوتي خيراً كثيراً و ما يذكر الا اولوا الالباب﴾ (البقرة/ 269)

"He grants wisdom to whom He pleases, and whoever is granted wisdom, he indeed is given a great good, and none but men of understanding mind."

(Sūrah 2: 269)

﴿الم تر انّ الله انزل من السماء ماءً فسلكه ينابيع في الارض ثم يخرج به زرعاً مختلفاً الوانه ثم يهيج فتريٰه مصفراً ثم يجعله حطاماً انّ في ذلك لذكري لاولي الالباب﴾ (الزمر/ 21)

"Do you not see that Allah sends down water from the cloud, then makes it go along in the earth in springs, then brings forth there with herbage of colours, then it withers so that you see it becoming yellow, then He makes it a thing crushed and broken into pieces? Most surely there is a reminder in this for the men of understanding."

(Sūrah 39: 21)

﴿لقد كان في قصصهم عبرة لاولي الالباب ...﴾ (يوسف/ 111)

"In their histories there is certainly a lesson for men of understanding."

(Sūrah 12: 111)

One can see that *'Ulul-Albāb* possess most of the characteristics mentioned in the Qur'an for understanding nature. They have purified intellects, and, therefore, have better capability for attaining a deeper knowledge of nature.

Also from the comparison of the following verses:

﴿و هوالذي جعل لكم النجوم لتهتدوا بها في ظلمات البرّ والبحر قد فصّلنا الآيات لقوم يعلمون﴾ (الانعام/ 97)

"And He it is who made the stars for you that you might follow the right way thereby in the darkness of the land and the sea; truly we have made plain the signs for people who know."

(Sūrah 6: 97)

﴿و هوالذي أنشأكم من نفس واحدة فمستقر و مستودع قد فصّلنا الآيات لقوم يفقهون﴾ (الانعام/ 98)

"And He it is who has brought you into being from a single soul, then there is (for you) a resting-place and a depository; indeed we have made plain the signs for a people who understand."

(Sūrah 6: 98)

﴿و هوالذي انزل من السماء ماء فاخرجنا به نبات كل شيئ فاخرجنا منه خضراً نخرج منه حبّا متراكباً و من النخل من طلعها قنوان دانية و جنات من اعناب والزيتون والرّمّان مشتبهاً و غيرمتشابه انظروا الى ثمره اذا اثمر و ينعه انّ في ذلكم لآيات لقوم يؤمنون﴾ (الانعام/ 99)

"And He it is who sends down water from the cloud, then We bring forth with it buds of all (plants), then we bring forth from it green (foliage) from which we produce grain piled up; and of the palm tree, of the sheaths of it, come forth clusters (of dates) within reach, ... most surely there are signs in this for a people who believe."

(Sūrah 6: 99)

we realise (as Allāmah Tabatabā'ī has mentioned)[126] that while understanding certain things related to plants is possible for unlearned believers, the understanding of astronomical problems requires scientific background, and the understanding of issues related to the human soul and its mysteries needs theoretical knowledge as well as profound understanding of human nature. The Qur'an refers to a sublime faculty of cognition which is the cognition of the 'spiritual dimension' (malakūt) of the heavens and the earth:

﴿و كذلك نري ابراهيم ملكوت السموات والارض وليكون من الموقنين﴾ (الانعام/ 75)

"And thus did We show 'Ibrāhīm the spiritual dimension of the heavens and the earth, and that he might be of those who are sure."

(Sūrah 6: 75)

﴿اولم ينظروا في ملكوت السموات والارض و ما خلق الله من شيئ ...﴾ (الاعراف/ 185)

"Do they not consider the spiritual dimension of the heavens and the earth and whatever things Allah has created?"

(Sūrah 7: 185)

Moreover, the first verse indicates that the vision of 'spiritual dimension' results in sureness. There have been various interpretations of *malakūt*. Some scholars, including Allāmah Tabatabā'i [127], believe it to be the innermost aspect of beings and the deepest attachment of their very existence to the Almighty God. Some mean by it wonders in the heavens and the earth[128], and some others interpret it as the laws of nature.[129]

In reference to the vision of '*Malakūt*', various views have been expressed. The majority of the interpreters believe it to be a non-sensual vision or an intellectual one[130]. Fakhr al-Dīn Rāzī in his interpretation of the first verse (i.e. 6: 75) says:

"There are two views in connection with the 'revealing': The First view indicates that God revealed the spiritual dimension to 'Ibrāhīm's ordinary eyes ... and the second indicates that it was his inner and mental discernment that had this vision, not his physical eyes. These things prove that the vision had been through mental discernment not through the eyes." [131]

It is quite certainly a profound cognition of nature; and as it ends in certitude and sureness, it is the highest level of cognition. But to attain this kind of cognition, one requires all the qualities mentioned in the verses quoted in this section.

Thus, we conclude that:

1. There are different levels for the understanding of a phenomenon.
2. For understanding different natural phenomena, there are different pre-requisite conditions.
3. To have a more profound understanding of nature, researchers should try to acquire the above-mentioned characteristics more and more. These characteristics can be briefly summarized in the following three categories: scientific aptitude, higher (analytical) intellect, and faith with piety.

One may question the role of faith and piety in the proper understanding of nature, asking for what reason has God denied the proper cognition to unbelievers in the following verses:

﴿قل انظروا ما ذا في السموات والارض و ما تغني الايات والنذر عن قوم لايؤمنون﴾ (يونس/ 101)

"Say consider what is that is in the heavens and the earth; and signs and warners do not avail a people who would not believe."

(Sūrah 10: 101)

﴿اولم يروا الي الارض كم انبتنا فيها من كل زوج كريم* انّ في ذلك لآية و ما كان اكثرهم مؤمنين﴾ (الشعراء/ 8-7)

"Do they not see the earth, how many of every noble kind we have caused to grow in it? Most surely there is a sign in that, but most of them will not believe."

(Sūrah 26: 7-8)

﴿و ما انت بهاد العمي عن ضلالتهم ان تسمع الّا من يؤمن بآياتنا فهم مسلمون﴾ (الروم/ 53)

"Nor can you lead away the blind out of their way. You cannot make to hear any but those who believe in our signs ..."

(Sūrah 30: 53)

Why has God attributed the understanding of some of his signs in nature to the believers and the pious only?

﴿انّ في السموات والارض لآيات للمؤمنين﴾ (الجاثية/ 3)

"Most surely in the heavens and the earth there are some signs for the believers."

(Sūrah 45: 3)

﴿انّ في اختلاف الليل والنهار و ماخلق الله في السموات و الارض لآيات لقوم يتقون﴾ (يونس/ 6)

"Most surely in the alternation of the night and the day and what Allah has created in the heavens and the earth, there are signs for a people who guard (against) evil."

(Sūrah 10: 6)

Is it not true that every person whether believer or non-believer many be capable of logical thinking? Isn't the Qur'an itself logically arguing with unbelievers and polytheists. To answer this question we seek help from the Qur'an itself. In view of the inseparability of piety and faith:

﴿... واتقوا الله ان كنتم مؤمنين﴾ (المائدة/ 57)

"And be careful of (your duty to) God if you are believers."

(Sūrah 5: 57)

﴿انْ تتقوا الله يجعل لكم فرقانا ...﴾ (الانفال/ 29)

one can point out that, as an effect of faith, man can differentiate between right and wrong, for his intellectual activity is free from the vices caused by devilish inducements and temptations. As Jalāl al-Dīn Rūmī puts it:

آينه دل چون شود صافى و پاك

نقش‌ها بينى برون از آب و خاك

هم ببينى نقش و هم نقاش را

فرش دولت را و هم فرّاش را

"When the mirror of heart gets clean and stainless,

Therein you see images beyond earth and water,

You see both the painter and the paintings,

Both the Divine carpet and the carpet spreader."

or as Hāfiz puts it:

چشم آلوده نظر از رخ جانان دوراست

بر رخ او نظر از آينة پاك انداز

غسل در اشك زدم كاهل طريقت گويند

پاك شو اوّل و پس ديده بر آن پاك انداز

"The blurred eye cannot reach the face of the beloved,

Cast your look upon her when your mirror is clean,

I rinsed my eyes clean with my own tears, as the visionaries say,

'First clean yourself and then look upon the clean'."

In his exegesis of the Qur'an, *al-Mīzān*, Allāmah Tabatabā'ī says:

"The reason why the Holy Qur'an emphasizes piety alongside reflection, intellection and remembrance, and has related knowledge with practice is that it ensures the stability of thought, righteousness of knowledge and avoidance of vices of caprice and evil." [132]

A saying from our great Prophet ﷺ has been reported, which confirms this:

﴿لولا انّ الشياطين يحومون علي قلوب بني آدم لنظروا الى ملكوت السماء﴾

"Had the party of devil not moved around the minds of the children of Adam, they would have seen the spiritual dimension of the sky." [133]

There is also a statement from Imam 'Alī (AS) on the same line [134]:

﴿و من لم يهذّب نفسه لم ينتفع بالعقل﴾

"One who does not render his heart clean does not benefit from his intellect."

Therefore, the important role of piety and cleanness of heart (sanctification) is to harness the slips of intellect. However, we deduct from certain Qur'anic verses and Islamic traditions that the effect of piety is not limited to the repulsion of the impediments of cognition; but through piety and sanctification one can attain cognition above and beyond the cognition attained through experience and reasoning. In this connection, we are going to cite some relevant verses from the Qur'an:

﴿... واتقوا الله و يعلمكم الله ...﴾ (البقرة/ 282)

"...and be careful of (your duty to) Allah and Allah teaches you...'

(Sūrah 2: 282)

﴿والذين جاهدوا فينا لنهدينهم سبلنا ...﴾ (العنكبوت/ 69)

"And (as for) those who strive hard for Us, We will most certainly guide them in Our ways ..."

(Sūrah 29: 69)

﴿و كذلك نري ابراهيم ملكوت السموات والارض وليكون من الموقنين﴾ (الانعام/ 75)

"And thus did We show 'Ibrāhīm the spiritual dimension (Malakūt) of the heavens and the earth, so that he might be of those who are sure."

(Sūrah 6: 75)

A tradition of the Prophet Muhammad ﷺ which is universally accepted and respected by all Muslims, says:

﴿قال رسول‌الله (ص): قال الله عزوجل ... وما تقرب الى عبد بشيئ احب اليّ مما افترضت عليه و انه ليتقرب اليّ بالنافلة حتي احبه فاذا احببته كنت سمعه الذي يسمع به و بصره الذي يبصربه ولسانه الذي ينطق به و يده التي يبطش بها انّ دعاتي اجبته و انّ سألني اعطيته﴾

"No servant has sought My proximity through what is more favourite to Me than performing his duties; but through praiseworthy acts a servant gets so close to Me that I love him. It is then that I become an ear for him by means of which he hears,

an eye for him by means of which he sees, a tongue for him by means of which he speaks and a hand with which he grasps. Should he call Me, I respond to him; and should he request something, I bestow upon him." [135]

It has also been reported that our great Prophet ﷺ had said:

﴿ما اخلص عبدالله عزوجل اربعين صباحا الا جرت ينابيع الحكمة من قلبه علي لسانه﴾

"No servant devotes his full forty mornings to (the service of) God except when the springs of wisdom flow from his heart to his tongue." [136]

and it is reported from Imam 'Alī (AS) in *Nahj al-Balāghah*:

﴿قد احيا عقله و امات نفسه حتي دق جليله و لطف غليظه و برق له لامع كثيرالبرق فابان له الطريق و سلك به السبيل، و تدافعته الابواب الي باب السلامة و دارالاقامة و ثبتت رجلاه بطمانينة بدنه في قرار الامن و الراحة، بما استعمل قلبه، وارضي ربه﴾

"He (the believer) kept his mind alive and killed (the desires of) his heart till his body became thin, his bulk turned light and effulgence of extreme brightness shone for him. It lighted the way for him and took him on the (right) path. Different doors led him to the door of safety and the place of (his permanent) stay. His feet, balancing his body, got fixed in the position of safety and comfort because he kept his heart busy (in good acts) and pleased his Allah." [137]

Also in *Nahj al-Balāghah* we find:

﴿هجم بهم العلم علي حقيقة البصيرة و باشروا روح اليقين واستلانوا ما استعوره المترفون و انسوا بما استوحش عنه الجاهلون﴾

"Knowledge has led them to real understanding and so they have associated themselves with the spirit of conviction. They take easy what the easy-going regard as hard. They love what the ignorant took as awful." [138]

In any case, it is certain that illumination and inspiration, as a source of knowledge is not open to all, and only those with proper background can benefit from it. The channel which is open to all is the employment of sensory experience and intellect; and, of course, in order to arrive at truth one should avoid the impediments in the way of cognition.

Impediments of Cognition

Sometimes, certain internal factors overrule the intellect, and prevent it from functioning properly. Then, while the judgements are said to have been made wisely, in fact they are the product of an unhealthy intellect polluted with impurities. As Allāmah Tabatabā'ī puts it:

"The role of intellect in such cases resembles that of a judge who passes an unjust verdict relying on (forged) documents or false witnesses, though he may not have intended to do so." [139]

Therefore, a researcher should shake his mind of unfounded prejudgements and suppositions, and cleanse it of immoralities, in order to attain a correct understanding. Al-Ghazzali in his book "*'Ihya 'Ulūm al-Dīn*" uses an interesting simile[140], which, in some respects casts light on this subject. He says that the human heart resembles a mirror which reflects good, clear pictures when it is shined and polished. The human heart, too, becomes more shining through noble qualities, and better reflects truth and realities; but when it is affected by vicious qualities, like a dust-covered mirror, it cannot depict realities. For the same reason, "not hearing" has connection with "the sealing of the heart" on account of faulty deeds as shown in the following verses of the Holy Qur'an:

﴿... لو نشاء أصبناهم بذنوبهم و نطبع علي قلوبهم فهم لايسمعون﴾
(الاعراف/ 100)

"If We please, We would afflict them on account of their faults, and set a seal on their hearts so they would not hear."

(Sūrah 7: 100)

﴿... واتقوا الله واسمعوا ...﴾ (المائدة/ 108)

"... And be careful of (your duty to) God and hear ..."

(Sūrah 5: 108)

Thus, listening to, and hearing the right word is connected with piety; and not hearing it, or sealing the heart, is connected with committing sins. Al-Ghazzali goes on with his simile and says:

For everything known there is a truth, a picture of which falls on the mirror of heart, which is the home of knowledge. Now, in the same way that an ordinary mirror cannot reflect an image because of any one of the following defects:

1. imperfect components
2. opacity of the face of the mirror
3. not facing the bright side of the mirror
4. the existence of a barrier between the mirror and the object
5. the object not being placed in front of the mirror.

A human heart, which is capable of understanding realities, may have that capacity affected by one of the following five causes:

1. intrinsic deficiency, as in the case of children
2. obscurity (darkness) caused by sins and lust

Therefore, turning one's face towards the Creator, and turning away from passions purifies the heart and makes it glitter:

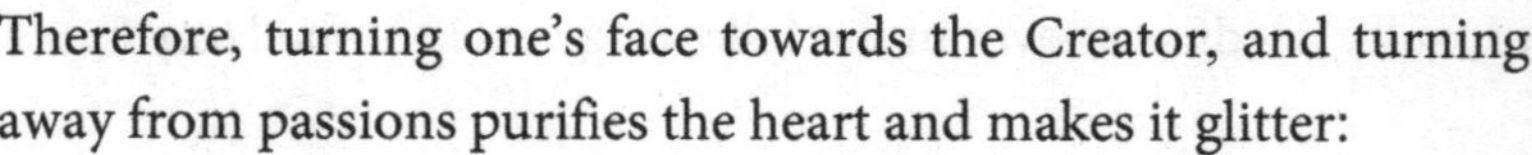

"Those who strive hard for us We will most certainly guide them in our ways ..."

(Sūrah 29: 69)

3. Not paying attention to realities

   A heart may be clean, but if it does not search for truth, the truth is not revealed to it. For instance, a man whose sole endeavour is physical worship or earning his livelihood, without any meditation on the Divine realities hidden from common man's eyes, may get only what he is after, not more.

4. The existence of obstacles in the way of cognizing realities, i.e. veils and barriers between the heart and the object in view, prevents access to the truth. Blind imitation of the ancestors and the sedimented opinions of one's own are hindrances to the perception of realities.

5. Ignorance of the method of attaining the object in view.

A man in search of knowledge cannot succeed to do so unless he is provided with the prerequisites for attaining the desired reality. Therefore, ignorance of these prerequisites and their manner of combination is an impediment in the way of attaining knowledge. For instance a man who wants to see the back of his head, but holds the mirror in front of him, cannot see what he wants; if he holds the mirror behind his head, he cannot see even the mirror, much less his back. Thus he needs two mirrors to achieve his purpose, and the two mirrors should be set in a special position in relation to each other. The same holds for cognition. For every cognition, its prerequisites should be attained first.

Ignorance creates the impediments between the heart and realities. Otherwise, the heart is intrinsically noble and capable of attaining realities (this is a brief summary of al-Ghazzali's views on the matter.)

Now we are going to cite from the Holy Qur'an the factors which prevent a correct cognition. These factors can be classified under two or three general headings, but for the sake of clarity of the matter, we use the very headings mentioned in the verses of the Qur'an.

1. Lack of faith

There are many verses in the Qur'an which indicate faithlessness as a great impediment in the way of cognition:

﴿ذلك بانّهم آمنوا ثم كفروا فطبع الله علي قلوبهم فهم لايفقهون﴾ (المنافقون/ 3)

"That is because they believe, then disbelieve, so a seal is set upon their hearts so that they do not understand."

(Sūrah 63: 3)

﴿وما انت بهاد العمي عن ضلالتهم ان تسمع الا من يؤمن بآياتنا فهم مسلمون﴾ (الروم/ 53)

"Nor can you lead away the blind out of their error. You cannot make to hear any but those who believe in our signs so they shall submit."

(Sūrah 30: 53)

﴿... كذلك يجعل الله الرجس علي الذين لايؤمنون﴾ (الانعام/ 125)

..."Thus does God lay uncleanness on those who do not believe."

(Sūrah 6: 125)

﴿... انّا جعلنا الشياطين اولياء الّذين لايؤمنون﴾ (الاعراف/ 27)

"Surly we have made the Shaitans to be guardians of those who do not believe,"

(Sūrah 7: 27)

﴿انّ الّذين لايؤمنون بآيات الله لايهديهم الله ...﴾ (النحل/ 104)

"(As for) those who do not believe in God's signs, surely God will not guide them."

(Sūrah 16: 104)

﴿... والّذين لايؤمنون في آذانهم وقر و هو عليهم عمىً ...﴾ (فصلت/ 44)

"... and (as for) those who do not believe, there is a heaviness in their ears and it is obscure to them."

(Sūrah 41: 44)

Some verses in the Qur'an indicate that the sole reliance on knowledge, without faith, can never take one to the correct understanding of nature:

﴿قل انظروا ماذا في السموات والارض و ما تغني الآيات و النذر عن قوم لايؤمنون﴾ (يونس/ 101)

"Say: consider what is it that is in the heavens and the earth; and signs and warners do not avail a people who would not believe."

(Sūrah 10: 101)

﴿فاعرض عن من تولي عن ذكرنا و لم يرد الّا الحيوة الدنيا ذلك مبلغهم من العلم انّ ربّك هو اعلم بمن ضلّ عن سبيله و هو اعلم بمن اهتدي﴾ (النجم/ 29-30)

"Therefore, turn aside from him who turns his back upon Our reminder and does not desire anything but this world's life. That is their goal of knowledge; and He knows best him who follows the right direction."

(Sūrah 53: 29-30)

As previously mentioned, the principal role of faith in understanding is to restore man's faculty of intellect to its original state.

2. The existence of the factors causing intellect's deviation

The existence of certain characteristics and qualities in some people prevents them from exercising sound judgement in discovering the truth. Here are some important ones:

a) *Following one's desires, fancies and wishes*

It is repeatedly mentioned in the Qur'an that following one's desires and wishes leads one astray:

﴿فان لم يستجيبوا لك فاعلم انّما يتبعون اهوائهم و من اضل ممن اتّبع هويه بغير هدي من الله ...﴾ (القصص/ 50)

"But if they do not answer you, know that they only follow their low desires: and who is more erring than he who follows his low desires without any guidance from Allah ..."

(Sūrah 28: 50)

﴿افرأيت من اتخذ الهه هويه واضلّه الله علي علم و ختم علي سمعه و قلبه و جعل علي بصره غشاوة فمن يهديه من بعد الله افلا تذكرون﴾ (الجاثية/ 23)

"Have you then considered him who takes his low desire for his God, and Allah has made him err, having knowledge, and has set a seal upon his ear and his heart and put a covering upon his

eye. Who can then guide him after Allah? Will you not then be mindful?"

(Sūrah 45: 23)

﴿... و لئن اتبعت أهواء هم بعد الذي جاءك من العلم مالك من الله من ولي و لانصير﴾ (البقرة/ 120)

"And if you follow their desires after the knowledge that has come to you, you shall have no guardian from Allah, nor any helper."

(Sūrah 2: 120)

﴿... فاحكم بين الناس بالحق و لاتتبع الهوي فيضلك عن سبيل الله ...﴾ (ص/ 26)

"... so judge between men with justice, and do not follow desire, lest it should lead you astray from the path of Allah."

(Sūrah 38: 26)

﴿... و انّ كثيراً ليضلون باهوائهم بغير علم ...﴾ (الانعام/ 119)

"... and most surely many would lead (people) astray by their low desires out of ignorance ..."

(Sūrah 6: 119)

﴿اولئك الذين طبع علي قلوبهم واتبعوا أهواءهم﴾ (محمد/ 16)

"And these are they upon whose hearts God has set a seal and they follow their low desires."

(Sūrah 47: 16)

Our great Prophet ﷺ has been quoted as saying:

﴿انّ اخوف ما اخاف علي امتّي الهوي و طول الامل، امّا الهوي فانّه

يصدّعن الحق، و امّا طول الامل فينسي الآخرة﴾.

"In your case I would fear of two characteristics: obedience to desires and indulgence. Obedience to desires and fancies keeps you away from finding truth, and indulgence causes you to forget the Hereafter." [141]

and it has been reported from Imam 'Alī (AS) as saying:

﴿الهوي عدوّ العقل﴾

"Desire is the enemy of reason." [142]

and

﴿الاماني تعمي اعين البصائر﴾

"Ambition blinds man's insight." [143]

b) *Blind love or hatred and unjustifiable prejudices*

These, too, are the factors which prevent the intellect from impartiality and seeking truth. As an Arab poet said:

و عين الرضا عن كل عيب كلية

و لكن عين السخط تبدي المساويا

"A look with satisfied eyes covers all the faults, but a look of discontent uncovers all the faults."

or as the Persian poet Jalāl al-Dīn Rūmī puts it:

چون غرض آمد هنر پوشیده شد

صد هزاران دل بهسوی دیده شد

"When bias comes, art is covered,

A hundred veils move from heart to (cover) the eyes. "

The Holy Qur'an has repeatedly warned man against the diseases which inflict the heart:

﴿و امّا ثمود فهديناهم فاستحبوا العمي علي الهدي فاخذتهم صاعقة العذاب الهون بما كانوا يكسبون﴾ (فصلت/ 17)

"And as to Thamūd, we showed them the right way, but they chose error above guidance, so there overtook them the scourge of an abasing chastisement for what they earned."

(Sūrah 41: 17)

﴿و عاداً و ثمود و قد تبيّن لكم من مساكنهم و زيّن لهم الشيطان اعمالهم، فصدّهم عن‌السبيل وكانوا مستبصرين﴾ (العنكبوت/ 38)

"And (we destroyed) 'Ād and Thamūd and from their dwellings (this) is apparent to you indeed; and the Shaytān (Satan) made their deeds fair seeming to them, so he kept them back from their path, though they were endowed with intelligence and skill."

(Sūrah 29: 38)

﴿... و قال يا قوم لقد ابلغتكم رسالة ربّي و نصحت لكم و لكن لا تحبّون الناصحين﴾ (الاعراف/ 79)

"Then said: O my people I did certainly deliver to you the message of my Lord, and I gave you good advice, but you do not love those who give good advice."

(Sūrah 7: 79)

﴿ذلك بانّهم استحبوا الحيوة الدنيا علي الآخرة وانّ الله لا يهدي القوم الكافرين اولئك الذين طبع الله علي قلوبهم و سمعهم و ابصارهم و اولئك هم الغافلون﴾ (النحل/ 107-108)

"This is because they have this world's life more than the Hereafter, and because Allah does not guide the unbelieving people. These are they on whose hearts and their hearing and their eyes Allah has set a seal, and these are the heedless ones."

(Sūrah 16: 107-108)

﴿لقد جئناكم بالحق و لكن اكثركم للحق كارهون﴾ (الزخرف/ 78)

"Certainly we have brought you the truth but most of you are adverse to the truth."

(Sūrah 43: 78)

﴿ذلك بانّهم كرهوا ما انزل الله فاحبط اعمالهم﴾ (محمد/ 9)

"That is because they hated what God revealed. So He rendered their deed null."

(Sūrah 47: 9)

﴿... و زيّن ذلك في قلوبكم و ظننتم ظنّ السوء و كنتم قوماً بوراً﴾ (الفتح/ 12)

..." and that was made fair seeming to your hearts and you thought an evil thought and you were a people to perish."

(Sūrah 48: 12)

﴿و قال نسوة في المدينة امرأة العزيز تراود فتاها عن نفسه قد شغفها حبّا انّا لنراها في ضلال مبين﴾ (يوسف/ 30)

"And women in the city said: "The chief's wife seeks her slave to yield himself (to her), surely he has affected her deeply with (his) love, most surely we see her in manifest error."

(Sūrah 12: 30)

﴿... و كذلك زين لفرعون سوء عمله و صدّعن السبيل ...﴾ (الغافر/ 37)

"And thus the evil of his deed was made fair seeming to Pharaoh, and he was turned away from the way ..."

(Sūrah 40: 37)

It has been quoted from our great Prophet ﷺ,

﴿حبّك للشيئ يعمي و يصم﴾

"Loving something makes you blind and deaf (in relation to it)."[144]

and it has been quoted from Imam 'Alī (AS):

﴿و من عشق شيئاً اعشي بصره و امرض قلبه فهو ينظر بعين غير صحيحة و يسمع باذن غير سميعة﴾

"A lover is blind and sick at heart, so he face the truth with unhealthy sight and a deaf ear." [145]

and:

﴿انّ القلب اذا كره عمي﴾

"Heart turns blind to what it dislikes." [146]

c) *Pomposity*

It often happens that a person (though aware of the fact) does not accept the truth. The Qur'an warns this group of people of God's severe punishment:

﴿يسمع آيات الله تتلي عليه ثم يصرّ مستكبراً كان لم يسمعها فبشّره بعذاب اليم و اذا علم من آياتنا شيئاً اتخذها هزواً اولئك لهم عذاب مهين﴾ (الجاثية/ 8-9)

"Who hears the communications of Allah recited to him, then persists proudly as though he has not heard them! So announce to him a painful punishment. And when he comes to know of any of Our communication, he takes it for a jest; these it is that shall have abasing chastisement."

(Sūrah 45: 8-9)

﴿فلما جاءتهم آياتنا مبصرة قالوا هذا سحر مبين و جحدوا بها واستيقنتها انفسهم ظلماً و علواً فانظر كيف كان عاقبة المفسدين﴾ (النمل/ 14-13)

"So when Our clear signs came to them, they said: this is clear enchantment, and they denied them unjustly and proudly while their soul had been convinced of them; consider, then how was the end of the mischief-makers."

(Sūrah 27: 13-14)

﴿... فما اغني عنهم سمعهم و لا ابصارهم و لا افئدتهم من شيئ اذ كانوا يجحدون بايات الله و حاق بهم ما كانوا به يستهزؤن﴾ (الاحقاف/ 26)

"But neither their ears nor their eyes, nor their hearts availed them anything since they denied the signs of God, and that which they mocked encompassed them."

(Sūrah 46: 26)

﴿انّ الذين كذّبوا باياتنا واستكبروا عنها لا تفتح لهم ابواب السماء ...﴾ (الاعراف/ 40)

"Surely (as for) those who reject Our signs and turn away from them haughtily, the doors of heaven shall not be opened for them."

(Sūrah 7: 40)

﴿و انّي كلّما دعوتهم لتغفرلهم جعلوا اصابعهم في اذانهم و استغشوا ثيابهم و اصرّوا واستكبروا استكباراً﴾ (نوح/ 7)

"And whenever I have called them that Thou mayest forgive them, they put their fingers in their ears, cover themselves with their garments, and persist and are puffed up with pride."

(Sūrah 71: 7)

﴿ثم ادبر واستكبر * فقال انّ هذا الّا سحر يؤثر﴾ (المدّثر/ 24-23)

"Then he turned back and was big with pride. Then he said: 'This is naught but enchantment narrated'."

(Sūrah 74: 23-24)

It is quoted from our Prophet ﷺ who said:

﴿يا علي ثلاث درجات و ثلاث كفارات و ثلاث منجيات ... و امّا المهلكات فشح مطاع و هوي متبع و اعجاب المرء بنفسه﴾.

"O, 'Ali, people perish because of three characteristics: jealousy, (carnal) desire, and egoism.' [147]

and it has been reported from Imam 'Alī (AS) who said:

﴿العجب يفسد العقل﴾

"Egoism corrupts intellect." [148]

d) *Blind imitation of the ancestors' opinions, men of authority, and the sediments of one's own thoughts*

These, too, are characteristics which put barriers in the way of seeking the truth, and are repeatedly condemned in the Qur'an:

﴿قالوا ربّنا انا اطعنا سادتنا و كبرائنا فاضلونا السبيلا﴾ (الاحزاب/ 67)

"And they shall say: O our Lord, Surely we obeyed our leaders and our great men, so they led us astray from the path."

(Sūrah 33: 67)

﴿... بل نتبع ما الفينا عليه ابائنا او لو كان اباؤهم لايعقلون شيئاً و لايهتدون﴾ (البقرة/ 170)

"Nay, we follow what we found our fathers upon. What, and though their fathers had no sense at all, nor did they follow the right way."

(Sūrah 2: 170)

﴿فلما جاءتهم رسلهم بالبينات فرحوا بما عندهم من العلم و حاق بهم ماكانوا به يستهزؤن﴾ (المؤمن/ 83)

"Then when their messengers came to them with clear arguments, they exulted in what they had with them of knowledge, and there beset them that which they used to mock."

(Sūrah 40: 83)

﴿و اذا قيل لهم تعالوا الى ما انزل الله و الى الرسول قالوا حسبنا ما وجدنا عليه ابائنا او لو كان اباؤهم لايعلمون شيئاً و لايهتدون﴾ (المائدة/ 104)

"And when it is said to them: follow what Allah has revealed and this messenger, they say: 'Nay! We follow what we find our fathers upon. What! and though their fathers had no sense at all, nor did they follow the right way."

(Sūrah 5: 104)

﴿و تلك عاد جحدوا بآيات ربّهم و عصوا رسله و اتبعوا امر كل جبّار

عنيد﴾ (هود/ 59)

"And this was 'Ād: they denied the signs of their Lord, and disobeyed His messengers and followed the bidding of every insolent opposer (of truth)."

(Sūrah 11: 59)

﴿... فاتبعوا أمر فرعون و ما أمر فرعون برشيد﴾ (هود/ 97)

"...but they followed the bidding of Pharaoh, and Pharaoh's bidding was not right-directing."

(Sūrah 11: 97)

e) *Haste in judgements*

Haste often is the cause of carelessness and error in understanding the truth. That is why the Qur'an has warned us against it:

﴿خلق الانسان من عجل سأوريكم آياتي فلا تستعجلون﴾ (الأنبياء / 37)

"Man is created of haste; now will I show to you my signs, therefore, do not ask Me to hasten (them) on."

(Sūrah 21: 37)

﴿يا ايهاالذين امنوا انّ جاءكم فاسق بنبأٍ فتبيّنوا انّ تصيبوا قوماً بجهالة فتصبحوا علي ما فعلتم نادمين﴾ (الحجرات/ 6)

"O you who believe! if an evil-doer comes to you with a report look carefully into it, lest you harm a people in ignorance, then be sorry for what you have done."

(Sūrah 49: 6)

It has been quoted from our Prophet ﷺ who said:

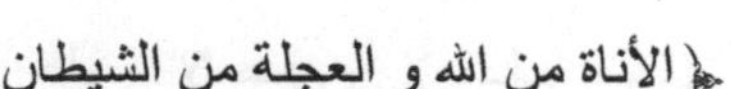

﴿الأناة من الله و العجلة من الشيطان﴾

"Haste is the deed of Shaytān and tranquility is from Allah." [149]

and Imam 'Alī (AS) has been quoted as saying:

﴿العجلة تمنع الاصابة﴾

"Haste hinders one from reaching righteousness and rectitude."[150]

3. Ignorance

Most of the errors in judgements (whether scientific or non-scientific) originate from ignorance of the subject and lack of enough knowledge about it.

In the Qur'an, there are a good number of verses in which ignorance has been condemned:

﴿قال ربّ اني اعوذبك ان اسألك ما ليس لي به علم ...﴾ (هود/ 47)

"He said: 'My Lord! I seek refuge in You from asking You that of which I have no knowledge'."

(Sūrah 11: 47)

﴿... فلم تحاجّون فيما ليس لكم به علم ...﴾ (آل‌عمران/ 66)

"why then do you dispute about that of which you have no knowledge?"

(Sūrah 3: 66)

﴿... و انّ كثيراً ليضلون باهوائهم بغير علم ...﴾ (الانعام/ 119)

"... And most surely many would lead (people) astray to their low desires out of ignorance ..."

(Sūrah 6: 119)

﴿و من الناس من يجادل في الله بغير علم و لا هدي و لا كتاب منير﴾
(الحج/ 8)

"And among men there is he who disputes about Allah without knowledge and without guidance and without an illuminating book."

(Sūrah 22: 8)

﴿... و ابلغكم ما ارسلت به و لكني اريكم قوماً تجهلون﴾ (الاحقاف/ 23)

"... and I deliver to you the message with which I am sent but I see you are a people who are ignorant."

(Sūrah 46: 23)

our great Prophet ﷺ is reported as saying:

﴿من افتي الناس بغير علم لعنته ملائكة السموات والارض﴾

"The angels in the heavens and the earth curse the person who passes judgement without knowledge."[151]

Among the evident examples of ignorant judgements, one may include subjection to conjecture, unfounded confirmations or rejections, and superficial consideration of events and phenomena.

a) *Subjection to conjecture*

In the Qur'an we have been repeatedly warned against subjection to conjecture and sacrificing knowledge to supposition:

﴿و قالوا ماهي الّا حياتنا الدنيا نموت و نحيا و ما يهلكنا الّا الدهر و ما لهم بذلك من علم ان هم الّا يظنّون﴾ (الجاثية/ 24)

"They say: there is nothing but our life in this world; we live and die and nothing destroys us but time, and they have no knowledge of that; they only conjecture."

(Sūrah 45: 24)

﴿و ما لهم به من علم ان يتبعون الا الظنّ و انّ الظنّ لا يغني من الحق شيئاً﴾ (النجم/ 28)

"And they have no knowledge of it; they do not follow anything but conjecture, and surely conjecture does not avail against the truth at all."

(Sūrah 53: 28)

﴿و ما يتّبع اكثرهم الا ظنّاً انّ الظنّ لا يغني من الحق شيئاً ...﴾ (يونس/ 36)

"And most of them do not follow (anything) but conjecture; surely conjecture will not avail against the truth."

(Sūrah 10: 36)

b) *Unfounded confirmations and rejections*

The glorious Qur'an encourages us to follow reason and avoid unfounded confirmations:

﴿... قل هل عندكم من علم فتخرجوه لنا ان تتبعون الا الظنّ و ان انتم الا تخرصون﴾ (الانعام/ 148)

"Say: 'Have you any knowledge with you so you should bring it forth to us? You only follow a conjecture and you only tell lies.'"

(Sūrah 6: 148)

﴿و قالوا لن يدخل الجنة الا من كان هوداً او نصاري تلك امانيهم قل هاتوا برهانكم ان كنتم صادقين﴾ (البقرة/ 111)

"And they said: None shall enter the garden (of paradise) except he who is a Jew or a Christian. These are their vain desires. Say: Bring your proof if you are truthful."

(Sūrah 2: 111)

﴿قل أرأيتم ما تدعون من دون الله اروني ماذا خلقوا من الارض ام لهم شرك في السموات ائتوني بكتاب من قبل هذا او أثارةٍ من علم ان كنتم صادقين﴾ (الاحقاف/ 4)

"Say: 'Have you considered what you call upon besides Allah? Show me what they have created of the earth, or have they a share in the heavens? Bring me a book (revealed) before this or traces of knowledge, if you are truthful'."

(Sūrah 46: 4)

﴿ان الذين يجادلون في آيات الله بغير سلطان اتيهم، ان في صدورهم الّا كبرما هم ببالغيه، فاستعذ بالله انه هو السميع البصير﴾ (غافر/ 56)

"Surely (as for) those who dispute about the signs of Allah without any authority that has come to them, there is naught in their breast but (a desire) to become great which they never attain to; therefore, seek refuge in Allah, surely He is the hearing, the seeing."

(Sūrah 40: 56)

﴿و لا تقف ما ليس لك به علم ان السمع والبصر والفؤاد كل اولئك كان عنه مسئولاً﴾ (الاسراء/ 36)

"And follow not that of which you have not the knowledge; surely the hearing and the sight and the heart, all of this shall be questioned about that."

(Sūrah 17: 36)

It is important, in any research, neither to confirm nor refute (reject) a view without taking into consideration all the relevant information available and even then one has to reserve judgement till one arrives at a certain result. It is quoted from

Imam al-Sādiq (AS) as having said:

﴿انّ الله تبارك و تعالي خصّ عباده بآيتين من كتابه ان لا يقولوا حتي يعلموا و لا يردوا ما لم يعلموا. قال الله عزوجل: ﴿الم يوخذ عليهم ميثاق الكتاب ان لا يقولوا علي الله الا الحق ...﴾ (الاعراف/ 169)، و قال: «بل كذبوا بمالم يحيطوا بعلمه و لما يأتهم تأويله ...﴾ (يونس/ 39)

"Allah has earmarked two verses from His Book (Qur'an) for his creatures: not to speak on any subject until they know about it, nor reject what they do not know. Allah has said: 'Did they not pledge not to utter but the truth about God.' and Allah has said: 'They rejected what they did not know while they had not access to its interpretation'." [152]

(Sūrah 10: 39)

Unfortunately, overlooking this important principle has led some research scholars in natural sciences to some unfounded generalisations or rejections, thus causing irreparable material and spiritual loss to human societies. Atheism and materialism, predominant in certain academic circles, are striking examples of this wrong attitude. Those who base their judgements on perceptibles alone have no right to deny supra-perceptible realities. The most they are entitled to do is to keep silent in such matters. Researchers should always bear in mind the advice given by Ibn Sina (Avicenna) in his *al-'Ishārāt wa al- Tanbīhāt* which in fact, beautifully elaborates the spirit of the aforementioned Qur'anic verses. It goes as follows:

"Lest you believe that rejecting is the sign of cleverness or disgusting vulgarity; because this is (a sign of) imbecility and weakness. Rejection of what is not clear to you is no less foolish than confirming what is not proved to you. Should you hear

something which sounds odd to you, you should hang onto it unless you have a proof for its improbability. It is advisable that you consider such issues just probable as long as they have not been rejected by firm proofs ..." [153]

c) *Superficiality*

The Qur'an strongly condemns those who look at the natural phenomena superficially and pass comments without trying to find reasons behind the natural events:

﴿و قالوا لو كنّا نسمع او نعقل ما كنّا في اصحاب السعير﴾ (الملك/ 10)

"*And they shall say: Had we but listened or ponder, we should not have not been among the inmates of the burning fire.*"

(Sūrah 67: 10)

﴿... و يجعل الرجس علي الذين لا يعقلون﴾ (يونس/ 100)

"*... and He casts uncleanness on those who will not understand.*"

(Sūrah 10: 100)

﴿و اذا ناديتم الى الصلوة اتخذوها هزواً و لعباً ذلك بأنّهم قوم لا يعقلون﴾ (المائدة/ 58)

"*And when you call to prayer they make mockery and a joke; this is because they are a people who do not understand.*"

(Sūrah 5: 58)

﴿و منهم من يستمعون اليك افانت تسمع الصّم و لو كانوا لا يعقلون﴾ (يونس/ 42)

"*And there are those of them who hear you, but can you make the deaf to hear though they will not understand?*"

(Sūrah 10: 42)

﴿افلم يسيروا في الارض فتكون لهم قلوب يعقلون بها ...﴾ (الحج/ 46)

"And have they not traveled in the land so that they should have hearts with which to understand, ..."

(Sūrah 22: 46)

﴿يعلمون ظاهراً من الحيوة الدنيا و هم عن الاخرة هم غافلون﴾ (الروم/ 7)

"They know the outward of this world's life, but of the Hereafter they are absolutely heedless."

(Sūrah 30: 7)

﴿و كاين من آية في السموات والارض يمرّون عليها و هم عنها معرضون﴾ (يوسف/ 105)

"And how many a sign in the heavens and the earth which they pass by, yet they turn aside from it."

(Sūrah 12: 105)

On the basis of the following two verses we can conclude that the fundamental difference between man and beasts of burden lies in rationality; therefore, a man not utilising his reason is even less conscious of the right way than animals:

﴿انّ شر الدواب عندالله الصمّ البكم الذين لا يعقلون﴾ (الانفال/ 22)

"Surely the vilest of animals, in Allah's sight, are the deaf, the dumb, who do not understand."

(Sūrah 8: 22)

﴿أم تحسب انّ اكثرهم يسمعون او يعقلون ان هم الّا كالانعام بل هم أضل سبيلاً﴾ (الفرقان/ 44)

"Or do you think that most of them do hear or understand? They are nothing but as cattle; nay, they are straying farther off from the path."

(Sūrah 25: 44)

4. Indifference toward craving for the truth

One of the important factors that leads a researcher, in any field of research, to success is that the researcher should solely look for the truth. The glorious Qur'an calls on man to seek and follow the truth:

﴿... فبشّر عباد الذين يستمعون القول فيتبعون احسنه اولئك الذين هديهم الله و اولئك هم اولوا الالباب﴾ (الزمر/ 18-17)

"... Therefore, give good news to My servants who listen to the word, then follow the best of it. These are whom Allah has guided and who are the men of understanding."

(Sūrah 39: 17-18)

﴿... افمن يهدي الي الحق احق ان يتبع امّن لا يهدي الّا ان يهدي ...﴾ (يونس/ 35)

"... Is He then Who guides to the truth more worth to be followed, or he who himself does not go aright unless he is guided?..."

(Sūrah 10: 35)

﴿... لقد جاءك الحق من ربك فلا تكونن من الممترين﴾ (يونس/ 94)

"... certainly the truth has come to you from your Lord, Therefore, you should not be of the disputers."

(Sūrah 10: 94)

﴿... فماذا بعد الحق الا الضلال فانّي تصرفون﴾ (يونس/ 32)

"... what is there after the truth but error; how are you then turned back?"

(Sūrah 10: 32)

Furthermore, the Qur'an condemns those who have no craving for truth or do not accept it when it is said to them:

﴿فقد كذّبوا بالحق لمّا جائهم ...﴾ (الانعام/ 5)

"So they have indeed rejected the truth when it came to them."

(Sūrah 6: 5)

﴿لقد جئناكم بالحق ولكن اكثركم للحق كارهون﴾ (الزخرف/ 78)

"Certainly we have brought you the truth, but most of you are adverse to the truth."

(Sūrah 43: 78)

﴿ومن اظلم ممن افتري علي الله كذباً او كذّب بالحق لمّا جاءه ...﴾ (العنكبوت/ 68)

"And who is more unjust than, one who forges a lie against Allah, or gives the lie to the truth when it has come to him ..."

(Sūrah 29: 68)

﴿ساصرف عن آياتي الذين يتكبرون فيالارض بغير الحق و ان يروا كلّ آية لا يؤمنوا بها و ان يروا سبيل الرشد لا يتخذوه سبيلاً و ان يروا سبيل الغي يتخذوه سبيلاً ذلك بانّهم كذبوا بآياتنا و كانوا عنها غافلين﴾ (الاعراف/ 146)

"I will turn away from my signs those who are unjustly proud in the earth; and if they see every sign they will not believe in it; and

if they see the way of rectitude they do not take it for a way, and if they see the way of error, they take it for a way. This is because they rejected our signs and were heedless of them."

(Sūrah 7: 146)

In the light of the glorious verses which follow, one comes to realise that Divine verses are instructive for the people who eagerly listen to and think about what they hear, and finally accept what is right: [154]

﴿و من آياته منامكم بالليل والنهار و ابتغاوكم من فضله انّ في ذلك لايات لقوم يسمعون﴾ (الروم/ 23)

"And one of His signs is your sleeping and your seeking of His grace by night and (by) day: most surely there are signs in this for people who would hear."

(Sūrah 30: 23)

﴿و الله انزل من السماء ماءً فاحيا به الارض بعد موتها انّ في ذلك لاية لقوم يسمعون﴾ (النحل/ 65)

"And Allah has sent down water from the heaven (cloud) and therewith given life to the earth after its death; most surely there is a sign in this for a people who would listen."

(Sūrah 16: 65)

Guiding Principles in Understanding Nature

We have already said that the Qur'an is not a book of natural science but a book of guidance and enlightenment, and wherever there is reference to the natural phenomena, it is meant to guide man through them. We also explained that God has gifted man with mental faculties so that through his own endeavours and God's help he can gradually come to understand the universe as well as his own self, and in that way to get nearer to the Creator of the universe.

According to the following glorious verses:

﴿... و نزّلنا عليك الكتاب تبياناً لكل شيئ و هدىً و رحمة و بشري للمسلمين﴾ (النحل/ 89)

"and we have revealed the book to you explaining clearly everything, and as a guidance and mercy and good news for those who submit."

(Sūrah 16: 89)

﴿... و ما فرّطنا في الكتاب من شيئ ...﴾ (الانعام/ 38)

"We have not neglected anything in the Book..."

(Sūrah 6: 38)

the Qur'an undertakes the guidance of human beings in all stages of life. One, therefore, can expect to derive the guiding principles for researches done in natural sciences from the Qur'an. By inference from the Qur'an we believe that, in addition to the principles of logic, such as the principle of "non-contradiction", the following principles too should be used as the guidelines for scientific research.

1. Faith in the principle of Divine unity (al-Tawhīd)

According to the Qur'anic verses, God is the only Creator and Ruler of the whole universe. Everything originates from Him and ends in Him. All creatures praise Allah, as the purpose behind the creation of man was to approach Allah through worshipping Him:

﴿و ما خلقت الجنّ و الانس الّا ليعبدون﴾ (الذاريات/ 56)

"And I have not created the jinn and the man except that they would worship Me."

(Sūrah 51: 56)

Hence, every step one takes should be aimed at gaining His consent and getting closer to the Almighty. The search for the discovery of nature is no exception to this rule. Observance of the grandeur in the Divine deeds, and making use of the possibilities therein for man to attain the eternal happiness should be given priority.

The Qur'an does not approve of such cognitions which aim at nothing except satisfying one's own curiosity. On the way of understanding nature, one should not busy oneself with the means and forget the ultimate end. If the researcher realises that God is Infinite in all respects, his attention to this infinite source keeps him moving on without hindrance, and he will be able to find more and more about the magnificence of creation. This is the surest way of attaining proximity to the Creator of the universe.

The understanding of nature should lead us along the road covered by prophet 'Ibrāhīm (Abraham), i.e,. commencing from the beginning of the string of causes and reaching the end – the Lord of the universe.

﴿فلما جَنّ عليه الليل رأي كوكبا قال هذا ربي فلمّا افل قال لا احب الافلين فلمّا رأي القمر بازغا قال هذا ربي فلمّا افل قال لئن لم يهدني ربي لاكونن من القوم الضالين فلمّا رأي الشمس بازغة قال هذا ربي هذا اكبر فلمّا افلت قال يا قوم انّي بري ممّا تشركون انّي وجّهت وجهي للذي فطر السموات و الارض حنيفا و ما انا من المشركين﴾ (الانعام/ 79-76)

"So when the night shadowed – over him, he saw a star, said he: Is this my Lord? So when it set, he said: I do not love the setting ones.' Then when he saw the moon rising, he said; 'Is this my

Lord?' So when it set, he said: 'if my Lords had not guided me I should certainly be of the erring people.' Then when he saw the sun rising, he said: 'Is this my Lord? Is this the greatest?' So when it set, he said: 'O my people! Surely I am clear of what you set up (with Allah). Surely I have turned myself, being upright, wholly to Him who originated the heavens and the earth, and I am not of the polytheists'."

(Sūrah 6: 76-79)

As a result, 'Ibrāhīm (AS) was led to see the spiritual dimension of the heavens and the earth:

﴿و كذلك نري ابراهيم ملكوت السموات و الارض و ليكون من الموقنين﴾

(الانعام/ 75)

"And thus did We show Ibrāhīm the spiritual dimension of the heavens and the earth and that he might be of those who are sure."

(Sūrah 6: 75)

and this is the way which all researchers have been invited to follow:

﴿اولم ينظروا في ملكوت السموات و الارض و ما خلق الله من شيئ ...﴾

(الاعراف/ 185)

"Do they not consider the spiritual dimension of the heavens and the earth and whatever things Allah has created..."

(Sūrah 7: 185)

A firm belief in monotheism arms the researcher with a comprehensive view of nature, not seeing it as a bundle of isolated pieces; rather, he observes their interrelations and their common origin, i.e., he sees a unity behind every multiplicity. Experiences of the past generations show that the scholars in the past always endeavoured to find a model according to which they could describe the whole nature. The Greeks had their designs for the explanation of the whole universe. In the Islamic world, too, different schools tried in different ways to discover a pattern for relating together various components of nature.

After the Renaissance, Newton tried to explain the celestial and terrestrial movements by the help of a series of laws. Then Einstein tried to take a step further than Newton in relation to natural issues. In the recent years, too, the main effort of the theoretical physicists has been to derive all the natural forces from one source. In all these stages it is quite apparent that the scientists have been trying to find suitable patterns by the help of which they could interpret all of the natural phenomena. They have been trying to generalise the result of an experiment carried out on the earth and apply it to the whole physical world.

This character of seeking for unification has been noticed among all scientists (whether materialist or non-materialist), and seems to be intrinsic to man. The difference between the two groups is that the former come to stop as soon as they reach the appearance; while the latter seek for the Coordinator of this harmonious system. Here we cite two glorious verses from the Qur'an: the first refers to the first group, while the second reveals the opinion of the second:

> 1. *"And they say: There is nothing but our life in this world; we live and die and nothing destroys us but time, and they have no knowledge of that; they only conjecture."*
>
> (Sūrah 45: 24)
>
> 2. *"He created the heavens and the earth in truth, highly exalted be He above what they associate (with Him)."*
>
> (Sūrah 16: 3)

An important point, which is greatly emphasised in the Qur'an, is the existence of order in natural phenomena, harmony among the various elements of nature, and a purpose in nature:

﴿... و كل شيئ عنده بمقدار﴾ (الرعد/ 8)

"And there is a measure with Him of everything."

(Sūrah 13: 8)

﴿... و خلق كل شيئ فقدّره تقديراً﴾ (الفرقان/ 2)

" And who created everything then ordained for it a measure."

(Sūrah 25: 2)

﴿... ما تري في خلق الرحمن من تفاوت فارجع البصر هل تري من فطور﴾ (الملك/ 3)

"... You see no incongruity in the creation of the Beneficent Allah, then look again, can you see any disorder?"

(Sūrah 67: 3)

The existence of this order and design is an indication of monotheism -the unity of the Almighty God:

﴿... لو كان فيها آلهة الا الله لفسدتا ...﴾ (الأنبياء / 22)

..."If there had been in them any gods except Allah, they would both have certainly been in a state of disorder."

(Sūrah 21: 22)

﴿... و ما كان معه من إله إذاً لذهب كل إله بما خلق و لعلا بعضهم علي بعض ...﴾ (المؤمنون/ 91)

"... and never was there with Him any (other) god - in that case would each god have certainly taken away what he created, and some of them would certainly have over-powered others..."

(Sūrah 23: 91)

﴿... صنع الله الذي اتقن كل شيئ ...﴾ (النمل/ 88)

"... the handiwork of Allah who has made everything thoroughly..."

(Sūrah 27: 88)

Belief in this principle is an important factor in encouraging scholars in their discovery of the laws of nature. In principle, any attempt to discover inter-relations in various aspects of nature without admitting order would look futile, as it would remain a local and temporary one.

A Belief in this principle makes us realise that wherever we failed to find the order in a natural phenomenon during our study, it would be due to the insufficiency of our knowledge rather than indicating the ruling of chance in nature.

During the early years of the second quarter of the twentieth century, when quantum mechanics was appearing, some of the pioneers of theoretical physics rejected the idea of the existence of order in the atomic domain. Einstein, though unable to present a successful alterative, was able to reject it by appealing to the principle of order in nature. In his letter to Max Born in December 1926, he wrote:

"Quantum mechanics is certainly imposing. But an inner voice tells me that it is not yet the real thing. The theory says a lot, but does not really bring us any closer to the secret of the "Old one". I, at any rate, am convinced that He is not playing at dice." [155]

In another letter to Born, in September 1944, he wrote:

"We have become Antipodean in our scientific expectations. You believe in the God who plays dice, and I in complete law and order in a world which objectively exists, and which I, in a wildly speculative way, am trying to capture. I firmly believe, but I hope that someone will discover a more realistic way, or rather a more

tangible basis than it has been my lot to find. Even the great initial success of the quantum theory does not make me believe in the fundamental dice-game, although I am well aware that our younger colleagues interpret this as a consequence of senility. No doubt the day will come when we will see whose instinctive attitude was the correct one." [156]

Despite their disbelief in monotheism, some philosophers believe in the existence of order in nature. But from our point of view, order, unity and co-ordination in nature can only be accounted for through the principle of monotheism (God's Oneness.)

Another conclusion drawn from the principle of monotheism is that the researcher, by observing the relation between the various aspects of nature, finds a unity among different branches of science and considers every one of them as a description of one dimension of the whole reality, and, therefore, does not reject any of them on the ground of his own unfamiliarity with it.

2. Belief in the reality of the external world

From the Qur'anic viewpoint, there is a real external world, indendent of our mind:

﴿و في الارض آيات للموقنين و في انفسكم افلا تبصرون﴾ (الذاريات/ 21-20)

"And in the earth there are signs for those who are sure, and in your own souls (too): will you not then see?"

(Sūrah 51: 20-21)

﴿لخلق السموات والارض أكبر من خلق الناس ولكن أكثر الناس لا يعلمون﴾ (المؤمن/ 57)

"Certainly the creation of the heavens and the earth is greater than the creation of the men, but most people do not know."

(Sūrah 40: 57)

﴿سبحان الذي خلق الازواج كلها ممّا تنبت الارض و من انفسهم و ممّا لا يعلمون﴾ (يس/ 36)

"Glory be to Him Who created pairs of all things, of what the earth grows, and of their kind and of what they do not know."

(Sūrah 36: 36)

﴿الذي جعل لكم الارض مهداً و جعل لكم فيها سبلا لعلكم تهتدون ... والذي خلق الازواج كلها و جعل لكم من الفلك و الانعام ما تركبون﴾ (الزخرف/ 12-10)

"He Who made the earth a resting place for you, and made in it ways for you that you may go aright ... And He Who created pairs of all things, and made for you of the ships and the cattle what you ride on."

(Sūrah 43: 10-12)

﴿و الله اخرجكم من بطون امهاتكم لا تعلمون شيئا و جعل لكم السمع والابصار و الافئدة ...﴾ (النحل/ 78)

"And Allah has brought you forth from the wombs of your mothers - you did not know anything – and He gave you the hearing and the sight and hearts..."

(Sūrah 16: 78)

﴿و تحسبهم ايقاظاً و هم رقود و نقلّبهم ذات اليمين و ذات الشمال و كلبهم باسط ذراعيه بالوصيد. لو اطلعت عليهم لوليّت منهم فرارا ولملئت منهم رعبا﴾ (الكهف/ 18)

"And you might think awake while they were asleep, and We turned them about to the right and to the left, while their dog (lay) outstretching its paws at the entrance; if you looked at them you would certainly turn back from them in flight, and you would certainly be filled with awe because of them."

(Sūrah 18: 18)

﴿و تري الجبال تحسبها جامدة و هي تمرّ مرّ الحساب ...﴾ (النحل/ 88)

"And you see the mountains, you think them to be sailed, and they shall pass away as the passing away of the cloud ..."

(Sūrah 27: 88)

﴿و ما يتبع اكثرهم الا ظنا ان الظن لا يغني من الحق شيئا ...﴾ (يونس/ 36)

"And most of them do not follow (anything) but conjecture; surely conjecture will not avail against the truth ..."

(Sūrah 10: 36)

These verses indicate that there exist realities other than and independent of our minds. If our mental image of a certain object does not correspond with the external reality, our mental image is not more than a fancy or imagination, which cannot lead us to reality.

Moreover, had there not been an external world, the Qur'an would not have so emphatically recommended the study of nature:

﴿قل سيروا في الارض فانظروا كيف بدأ الخلق ...﴾ (العنكبوت/ 20)

"Say: travel in the earth and see how He makes the first creation..."

(Sūrah 29: 20)

﴿قل انظروا ماذا في السموات والارض ...﴾ (يويس/ 101)

"Say: look and see what there are in the heaven and the earth…"

(Sūrah 10: 101)

﴿اولم ينظروا في ملكوت السموات والارض و ما خلق الله من شيئ ...﴾ (الاعراف/ 185)

"Do they not consider the spiritual dimension of the heavens and the earth and whatever things Allah has created."

(Sūrah 7: 185)

Belief in the reality of the external world is the basis of all researches in all of the empirical sciences, and without it any scientific research would be only a mental exercise. As Einstein puts it in his commemorative paper on Maxwell:

> *"The belief in an external world independent of the perceiving subject is the basis of all natural sciences."* [157]

3. Faith in supra-physical reality and limitation of human knowledge

In this respect, we learn the following points from the Holy Qur'an:

a) *Human knowledge is limited:*

﴿و ما اوتيتم من العلم الا قليلا﴾ (الاسراء/ 85)

"And you are not given aught of knowledge but a little."

(Sūrah 17: 85)

﴿سبحان الذي خلق الازواج كلّها ممّا تنبت الارض و من انفسهم و ممّا لا يعلمون﴾ (يس/ 36)

"Glory be to Him who created pairs of all things of what the earth grows, and of their kind and of what they do not know."

(Sūrah 36: 36)

﴿والخيل والبغال والحمير لتركبوها و زينة و يخلق ما لا تعلمون﴾ (النحل/ 8)

"And (He made) horses and mules and asses that you do ride upon them and as an ornament; and He creates what you do not know."

(Sūrah 16: 8)

b) There are many things we cannot get through our senses:

﴿فلا أقسم بما تبصرون و ما لا تبصرون﴾ (الحاقة/ 39-38)

"I swear by what you see and what you don't see."

(Sūrah 69: 38-39)

﴿الله الذي رفع السموات بغير عمد ترونها ...﴾ (الرعد/ 2)

"Allah is He Who roused the heavens without any pillars that you see, and He is firm in power ..."

(Sūrah 13: 2)

c) We should believe in the occult, i.e., in supernatural realities[158]*:*

﴿ذلك الكتاب لا ريب فيه هدى للمتقين الذين يؤمنون بالغيب و يقيمون الصلاة و ممّا رزقنا هم ينفقون﴾ (البقرة/ 3-2)

"This book, there is no doubt in it, is a guide to those who guard (against evil). Those who believe in the occult and keep up prayer and spend out of what We have given them."

(Sūrah 2: 2-3)

The faith in the limitation of human knowledge and the metaphysical realities leads us to the following corollaries:

1. Never to think we have discovered everything. Of course, this by no means indicates that man will not be able to discover any of the truths in the world, but we should not claim to have a full understanding of a natural phenomenon at a certain time. Sayyid Qutb in his interpretation of the verse 3 of the chapter *al-Baqarah* says:

> *"Faith in the supra-physical is a stage by attaining which man rises above the level of animality – at which perception is confined to the domain of external senses – and reaches the stage of humanity, a much larger and more spacious domain beyond the limited domain of external senses opens up before him. The transference to this new stage brings a radical change in man's view of the reality of existence in general, and his own self in particular. And he perceives hidden powers in the universe; how, he is greatly affected by a new feeling and can perceive in the creation the Power and Wisdom at work behind it. This transference affects the realities of one's life, because there is a great difference between a person whose life is entrenched in the limited span of sensory perception and the one whose soul and insight take him to the vast kingdom (of higher realities) where he can hear and feel the mysterious music and inspiration gushes out of the depths of his heart. He feels that the extent of the universe is too great for him to comprehend during his short span of life. He realises that beyond the seen and unseen universe of existence, there exists a truth much greater than existence and He is the Creator and the Preserver of it. This truth is not visible to human eye and is not discerned by human wisdom alone.*
>
> *This feeling (knowledge of the immensity of the unknown) safeguards the limited human faculty of thinking and does not*

let it go astray and waste itself in the areas for which it has not been created." [159]

4. Belief in the principle of general causality

The principle of causality says that every event requires a cause. This principle has two important corollaries:

a) The Principle of Determinism: any effect requires a cause, and without a cause it is impossible to have an effect.

b) The Principle of Uniformity of Nature: similar causes entail similar effects.

These two corollaries are inseparable from the principle of general causality, and any violation in them will be the violation of the principle of general causality.[160]

After this brief introduction, we want to demonstrate that the Qur'an admits the principle of general causality:

a) In the Qur'an we have many verses which talk of unchangeable patterns (*sunan*) of Allah in the universe:

﴿سنة من قد ارسلنا قبلك من رسلنا و لا تجد لسنتنا تحويلا﴾ (الاسراء/ 77)

"(This is Our) course with regard to those of Our messengers whom We sent before you, and you shall not find a change in our course."

(Sūrah 17: 77)

﴿سنة الله في الذين خلوا من قبل و لن تجد لسنة الله تبديلا﴾ (الاحزاب/ 62)

"(Such has been) the course of Allah with respect to those who have gone before; and you shall not find any change in the course of Allah."

(Sūrah 33: 62)

﴿ما كان علي النبي من حرج فيما فرض الله له سنة الله في الذين خلوا من قبل و كان امر الله قدراً مقدورا﴾ (الاحزاب/ 38)

"There is no harm in the prophet doing that which Allah has ordained for him; such has been the course of Allah with respect to those who have gone before; and the command of Allah is a decree that is made absolute."

(Sūrah 33: 38)

﴿يريد الله ليبين لكم و يهديكم سنن الذين من قبلكم ...﴾ (النساء/ 26)

"Allah desires to explain to you, and to guide you into the ways of those before you ..."

(Sūrah 4: 26)

We find many examples of these patterns in the Qur'an itself:

﴿ ...انّ الله لا يغير ما بقوم حتي يغيروا ما بانفسهم... ﴾ (الرعد/ 11)

"... Most surely Allah does not change the condition of a people until they change their own condition."

(Sūrah 13: 11)

﴿و اذا اردنا ان نهلك قرية امرنا مترفيها ففسقوا فيها ... فدمّرناها تدميرا﴾ (الاسراء/ 16)

"And when We wish to destroy a town, we send Our commandment to the people of it who lead easy lives; but they transgress therein ... So We destroy it with utter destruction."

(Sūrah 17: 16)

﴿وعدالله الذين امنوا منكم و عملوا الصالحات ليستخلفنّهم في الارض ...﴾ (النور/ 55)

"Allah has promised to those of you who believe and do good that We most certainly make them rulers in the earth ..."

(Sūrah 24: 55)

﴿و لا تهنوا و لا تحزنوا و انتم الاعلون ان كنتم مؤمنين... ﴾ (آل‌عمران/ 139)

"And be not infirm, and be not grieving, and you shall have the upper hand if you are believers."

(Sūrah 3: 139)

﴿و ما كان ربك ليهلك القري بظلم و اهلها مصلحون﴾ (هود/ 117)

"And it did not beseem your Lord to have destroyed the towns tyrannously, while their people acted well."

(Sūrah 11: 117)

﴿... فأما الزبد فيذهب جفاء و اما ما ينفع الناس فيمكث في الارض ...﴾ (الرعد/ 17)

"... then as for the scum, it passes away as a worthless thing; and as for that which profits the people, it tarries in the earth..."

(Sūrah 13: 17)

﴿... و لا يحيق المكر السيئ الا باهله فهل ينظرون الا سنة الاولين فلن تجد لسنةالله تبديلا و لن تجد لسنةالله تحويلا ﴾ (فاطر/ 43)

"... and the evil plans shall not beset any save the authors of it. Then should they wait for aught except the former people? For you shall not find any alteration in the course of Allah; and you shall not find any change in the course of Allah."

(Sūrah 35: 43)

b) Some of the Qur'anic verses indicate that both the creation and the course of events in nature follow a certain measure, and every natural being has a definite and precise life span:

﴿ الشمس و القمر بحسبان ﴾ (الرحمن/ 5)

"The sun and the moon follow a reckoning. "

(Sūrah 55: 5)

﴿و ان من شيئ الّا عندنا خزائنه و ما ننزله الّا بقدر معلوم﴾ (الحجر/ 21)

"And there is not a thing but with Us are the treasures of it, and we do not send it down but in a knowing measure."

(Sūrah 15: 21)

﴿ ...و كل شيئ عنده بمقدار ﴾ (الرعد/ 8)

"... and there is a measure with Him of everything."

(Sūrah 13: 8)

﴿أولم يتفكروا في انفسهم ما خلق الله السموات والارض و ما بينهما الّا بالحق و اجل مسمي و ان كثيرا من الناس بلقاء ربهم لكافرون﴾ (الروم/ 8)

"Do they not reflect within themselves: Allah did not create the heavens the heavens and the earth and what is between them but with truth, and (for) an appointed term? And most surely most of the people are deniers of the meeting of their Lord?"

(Sūrah 30: 8)

c) Some verses mention the mechanism and the specific course of certain events in nature:

﴿و لقد خلقنا الانسان من سلالة من طين ثم جعلناه نطفة في قرار مكين ... ﴾ (المؤمنون/ 13-12)

"and certainly We created man of an extract of clay, then we made a small life-germ in a firm resting place ..."

(Sūrah 23: 12-13)

﴿و انزل من السماء ماءً فاخرج به من الثمرات رزقا لكم... ﴾ (البقرة/ 22)

"And (Who) sends down rain from the cloud, then brings forth with it subsistence for you ..."

(Sūrah 2: 22)

﴿ ... قال ابراهيم فان الله يأتي بالشمس من المشرق فأت بها من المغرب فبهت الذي كفر... ﴾ (البقرة/ 258)

"... Ibrāhīm said: so surely Allah causes the sun to rise from the east. Then make it rise from the west. Thus he who disbelieved was confounded..."

(Sūrah 2: 258)

﴿وَ الشمس تجري لمستقرلها ذلك تقدير العزيز العليم والقمر قدرناه منازل حتي عاد كالعرجون القديم لا الشمس ينبغي لها ان تدرك القمر و لا الليل سابق النهار و كل في فلك يسبحون﴾ (يس/ 40-38)

"And the sun runs on to a term appointed for it, that is the ordinance of the mighty, the knowing. And (as for) the moon, We have ordained for it stages till it becomes again as an old dry palm branch. Neither is it allowable to the sun that it should overtake the moon, nor can the night outstrip the day; and all of them float through space."

(Sūrah 36: 38-40)

d) Some verses talk of the role of certain intermediary causes in the occurrence of some events:

﴿و ارسل عليهم طيرا ابابيل ترميهم بحجارة من سجيل﴾ (الفيل/ 4-3)

"And sent down (to prey) upon them birds in flocks, casting them against stones of baked clay."

(Sūrah 105: 3-4)

﴿و الله انزل من السماء ماءً فأحيا به الارض بعد موتها... ﴾ (النحل/ 65)

"And Allah has sent down water from the cloud and there with given life to the earth after its death ..."

(Sūrah 16: 65)

﴿و من الثمرات النخيل والاعناب تتخذون منه سكراً و رزقاً حسنا... ﴾ (النخل/ 67)

"And of the fruits of the palms and the grapes – you obtain from them intoxication and goodly provision."

(Sūrah 16: 67)

﴿و ارسلنا الرياح لواقح... ﴾ (الحجر/ 22)

"And We send the winds fertilizing ..."

(Sūrah 15: 22)

﴿و قاتلوهم يعذبهم الله بايديكم و يخزهم و ينصركم عليهم و يشف صدور قوم مؤمنين﴾ (التوبة/ 14)

"Fight them; Allah will punish them by your hands and bring them to disgrace, and assist you against them and heal the hearts of a believing people."

(Sūrah 9: 14)

These verses show that certain definite laws rule over the universe. This however, is meaningful only if the principle of general causality is valid. In this case every event stands in its definite place, i.e. every event appears under definite conditions and at a definite time and place. This does not imply that events are independent of the Almighty's Will and order, but it means that everything is realised by God's Will, but through a special channel. Verses of the following type confirm this view:

﴿و البلد الطيب يخرج نباته باذن ربه والذي خبث لا يخرج الا نكدا... ﴾
(الاعراف/ 58)

"And as for the good land, its vegetation springs forth (abundantly) by the permission of its Lord, and (as for) that which is inferior (its herbage) comes forth but scantly."

(Sūrah 7: 58)

﴿قد جاءكم من الله نور و كتاب مبين يهدي به الله من اتبع رضوانه سبل السلام و يخرجهم من الظلمات الى النور باذنه ﴾... (المائدة/ 16-15)

"Indeed, there has come to you light and a clear book from Allah. With it Allah guides him who will follow His pleasure into the ways of safety and brings them out of utter darkness into light by His will..."

(Sūrah 5: 15-16)

The first verse indicates that although God's Will is necessary for the growth of plants, yet the suitability of the land is also a condition. Not every sort of plant can be raised in every piece of land. With the suitability of the land God makes it possible for the plant to grow.

It can be also deduced from the verses 15-16 of the chapter *Mā'idah* (food) that only those seeking God's consent would enjoy His guidance in the Qur'an.

Some well-known Muslim theologians, particularly of *Ash'arītes* school, on the basis of verses like:

﴿... قل الله خالق كل شيئ و هو الواحد القهار﴾ (الرعد/ 16)

"Say: Allah is the Creator of all thing, and He is the One, the Supreme."

(Sūrah 13: 16)

﴿و الله خلقكم و ما تعملون﴾ (الصافات/ 96)

"And Allah has created you and what you make."

(Sūrah 37: 96)

﴿...الا له الخلق و الامر...﴾ (الاعراف/ 54)

"... Surely His is the creation and command ..."

(Sūrah 7: 54)

﴿...بل لله الامر جميعا...﴾ (الرعد/ 31)

"... The commandment is wholly Allah's ..."

(Sūrah 13: 31)

﴿أفرأيتم ما تحرثون ءأنتم تزرعونه ام نحن الزارعون﴾ (الواقعة/ 64-63)

"Have you considered what you saw? Is it you that cause it to grow or are We the causes of growth?"

(Sūrah 56: 63-64)

which attribute creation and governance of the universe to Allah, and verses like:

﴿قلنا يا نار كوني برداً و سلاماً علي ابراهيم﴾ (الأنبياء / 69)

"We said: O fire! be a comfort and peace to Ibrāhīm."

(Sūrah 21: 69)

which are indicative of the possibility of miracles, have rejected the law of causation in the physical world and say that physical means have no role in the realization of a phenomenon. The cause of any occurrence is God's Will, except that it is God's way to create what we call "effect" after what we call "cause", without any relation between them that necessitates the effect to follow the cause. They say: It is not fire which causes the cotton to burn; rather, it is Allah who makes the cotton burn and turns it into ashes; and of course, if God does not want, the fire will not burn the cotton. Al-Ghazzali, a chief representative of *Ash'arīsm*, says in his book *Tahāfut al-Falāsifah*:

> *"According to us, the connection between what is usually believed to be a cause and what is believed to be an effect is not a necessary connection. In the case of two things which are not identical and the affirmation or negation of one is not implied in the affirmation or negation of the other, neither the existence, nor the non-existence of the one necessitates the existence or the non-existence of the other. For example, the satisfaction of thirst does not imply drinking, nor satiety, eating, nor burning, contact with fire, nor light, sunrise, nor decapitation, death, nor recovery, taking of medicine, nor evacuation, the taking of a purgative, and so on for all the empirical connections existing in medicine, astronomy, the sciences and the crafts.*
>
> *For the connections in these things are based on a prior power of God to create them in a successive order, though not because this connection is necessary in itself and cannot be disjoined. On the contrary, it is God's power to create satiety without eating, and death without decapitation, and to let life persist notwithstanding the decapitation, and so on with respect to all connections.*
>
> *The philosophers, however, deny this possibility and claim that it is impossible to investigate all these innumerable connections*

would take too long, and so we shall choose one single example, namely the burning of cotton through contact with fire; for we regard it as possible that the contact might occur without burning taking place, and also that the cotton might be changed into ashes without any contact with fire, although the philosophers deny this possibility.

It is God who made the cotton burn and made it ashes either through intermediation of angels or without intermediation. For fire is a dead body which has no action and what is the proof that it is the agent? Indeed, the philosophers have no other proof than the observation of the occurrence of the burning, when there is contact with fire, but observation proves only a simultaneity, not a causation, and in reality, there is no other cause but God." [161]

This theory is rooted in the idea that accepting a decisive order in the world would require the denial of God's power. Muslim philosophers reject the *Ash'arīte* view and say:

a) The coincidence of two causes operating on a single object is impossible only when the two causes operate transversally, whereas the longitudinal operation of two causes on the same object is quite possible.[162] If we believe in the longitudinal system of causes, we could relate every occurrence to God; because He gives it existence. This emanation, however, takes place through special channels. That is the reason why God attributes the regulating of affairs sometimes to Himself and sometimes to the angels:

﴿يدبر الامر من السماء الي الارض... ﴾ (السجدة/ 5)

"He regulates the affairs from the heaven to the earth ..."

(Sūrah 32: 5)

﴿فالمدبرات امرا﴾ (النازعات/ 5)

"By those who regulate an affair"

(Sūrah 79: 5)

He also attributes taking of souls to Himself or to angels:

﴿الله يتوفي الانفس حين موتها ... ﴾ (الزمر/ 42)

"Allah takes the souls at the time of their death ..."

(Sūrah 39: 42)

﴿قل يتوفيكم ملك الموت الذي وكّل بكم... ﴾ (السجدة/ 11)

"Say: the angel of death who is given charge of you shall cause you to die ..."

(Sūrah 32: 11)

b) In the case of material bodies, what is commonly called "cause" is not the efficient cause but it is an intermediary or preparing cause which prepares the ground for God's bounty. These causes are materialistic and preparatory requirements for an event to occur, and are sometimes interpreted as the transversal system of causes. So, one can say that God is the cause for everything, but he makes everything under certain terms and through certain means; and of course, all these means and ways are the objects made by the Almighty Himself. Sadr al-Dīn Shīrāzī explains Muslim philosophers' view in the following way:

"Another group of philosophers and some elite among our Imamiah scholars say that objects vary in their acceptance of existence from the Origin. Some do not yield to existence unless another being precedes them, in the same way that accident should follow substance. Thus the Creator, whose power is

unlimited, grants the existence according to the possibilities through a particular order and in consideration of its various capabilities. Some come directly from Him, some through an intermediary or intermediaries. In the last case, nothing can come into existence unless its means and pre-requisites come into reality. God Himself is the Cause without a cause. Requirements for existence are not the result of deficiency in the Almighty's power, but due to weakness in the receiver of emanation. How can one imagine any need or deficiency in the Creator, while means and ways are all originated from Him? Therefore, the Glorious God does not need any help in the creation of anything." [163]

Thus, verses of the following type:

﴿افرايتم ما تحرثون ءأنتم تزرعونه ام نحن الزارعون لو نشاء لجعلناه حطاماً فظلتم تفكهون ... أفرايتم الماء الذي تشربون ءأنتم انزلتموه من المزن ام نحن المنزلون لو نشاء لجعلناه اجاجا فلولا تشكرون﴾ (الواقعة/ 70-63)

"Have you considered what you saw? Is it you that cause it to grow, or are We the cause of growth? If We pleased, We should have certainly made it broken down into pieces, then would you begin to lament ... Have you considered the water which you drink? Is it you that send it down from the clouds, or are We the senders? If We pleased, We would have made it saltish; why do you not then give thanks?"

(Sūrah 56: 63-70)

Which have been used as the basis of reasoning by Imam Fakhr al-Dīn Rāzī [164] in the rejection of the system of cause and effect do not indicate the negation of intermediary means in the occurrence of natural phenomena, but they indicate that we should not stop at the channels of emanation and should not remain unaware of the main cause who is the Commander (Ruler) of the whole universe, life giver to all, and He who is at the head of the longitudinal system of all causes, nor should we think that these are self-activating. As the late Dr. Beheshtī puts it:

"The fact is that Holy Qur'an wants to guide man from this end of the cord, i.e. sensibles, to the other end of the cord which is Allah. It wants that man does not stop at intermediary causes and fail in reaching the Origin. In all of the verses there is a voice which says: 'Be alert', while you are studying this world, don't slip into a ditch; take care not to leave the cord; do not drown yourself in the world of matter or contingents ... It is true that for agriculture you make preparations, which you should, but do not imagine that the cord is fully in your hand. Do you not see that at times you find a green sapling suddenly dies and fades despite the utmost care and with all the modern and old means that you employ to make it grow? Thus you, with all the means that you have at your disposal, are too insignificant to have the end of the cord. It is true that your drinking water comes down from the clouds, but do not let your keen eye to linger on the cloud saying that the water in the cloud is pure. The Qur'an says: it may rain, but the rain might be so badly contaminated or bitter and distasteful that one could not drink a drop of it; so the end of the cord of your drinking water is not in the hand of the cloud, but in the hand of the Wise Omnipotent, Who has created clouds and hundreds of other agents which work under His command and furnish men with fresh tasty water."[165]

In the case of miracles, too, considering the invariability of Divine patterns in nature, we do not find it necessary to look for the exceptions in the laws of nature; because if we find a deviation from a natural law, this does not necessarily means that the law is not correct or that the law of causality is violated. Because it is possible to make one law ineffective by the help of another law in the universe. If a body falls because of gravity, this force may be neutralised by the use of another force. Therefore, on the observance of a suspended body in the air, we should not immediately suppose that there is no such law as gravitation; rather, we can assume that there is another force besides the force of gravity. As the late Iranian philosopher Murtadā Mutahharī put it:

> *"Neither do the laws of creation yield themselves to exceptions, nor are miracles exceptional deeds in the laws of creation. If we observe certain changes in the patterns of the universe, it is because of the interference of other patterns or laws, which, they too, have general validity under their own special conditions. That is, one law does not change without the effect of another law. In the universe, all the laws, courses and patterns are invariable. If a dead (man) comes back to life, it follows a law of its own; if a son is born without having a father – as in the case of Īsā son of Maryam (Jesus Christ) – that, too, is not against Allah's course or the laws of the universe; the problem is that man does not know all the patterns and laws of the universe, and what he knows as a law, in many cases has the appearance of a law and is not a real one."* [166]

After the appearance of the quantum theory in physics, and the presentation of the principle of uncertainty by W. Heisenberg in the early years of the second quarter of the present century, some of the founders of this theory denied the existence of causal system in the world of particles and permitted the rejection of the principle of uniformity of nature and the principle of determinism, and gave a statistical status to the laws of microphysics. Most of the physicists, with the exception of some prominent ones likes Planck and Einstein, raised their voices in favour of the new theory and more or less accepted its orthodox interpretation, a situation which is still going on, although the lapse of time has increased the number of opponents.

Einstein and his colleagues rejected this theory because they could not accept that probabilities were ruling over the universe. From their viewpoint, the objective of physics should be to explain all natural phenomena according to absolute laws. The reason why we stick to statistical laws is that we are either ignorant of absolute laws which are the basis of statistical laws, or we are dealing with innumerable particles forcing us stick to statistical mathematics for the sake of simplification. As Einstein put it in his 1933 lecture at oxford:

> *"I cannot but confess that I attach only a transitory importance to this interpretation. I still believe in the possibility of a model of reality – that is to say, of a theory which represents things themselves and not merely the probability of their occurrence."* [167]

In a letter addressed to Born in April 1924 Einstein wrote:

> *"... I should not want to be forced into abandoning strict causality without defending it more strongly than I have so far. I find the idea quite intolerable that an electron exposed to radiation should choose of its own free will, not only its moment to jump off, but also its direction. In that case, I would rather be a cobbler, or even an employee in a gambling house, rather than a physicist. Certainly my attempts to give tangible form to the quanta have foundered again and again, but I am far from giving up hope. And even if it never works there is always that consolation that this lack of success is entirely mine."* [168]

In recent years we come across some Muslim scholars[169] who have revived the forsaken theory of the Muslim theologians following *Asharite* school, citing the quantum theory as a proof for their claims. To answer them, we are going to quote Dirac, who was one of the founders of quantum physics. In a recent paper (1979) he said:

"It seems clear that the present quantum mechanics is not in its final form. Some further changes will be needed, just about as drastic as the changes which one made in passing from Bohr's orbits to quantum mechanics. Some day a new relativistic quantum mechanics will be discovered in which we don't have these infinities occurring at all. It might very well be that the new quantum mechanics will have determinism in the way that Einstein wanted. This determinism will be introduced only at the expense of abandoning some other preconceptions which physicists now hold, and which it is not sensible to try to get at now.

So under these conditions I think it is very likely, or at any rate quite possible, that in the long run Einstein will turn out to be correct, even though for the time being, physicists have to accept the Bohr probability interpretation - specially if they have examinations in front of them." [170]

Finally, in confuting those who deny the validity of the principle of causality in the atomic and sub-atomic domain, we say:

a) If we deny the validity of the principle of causality in the atomic and sub-atomic world, this would mean defacing this principle in relation to the whole world, because causality brings the whole world together. As the Persian mystic Shaikh Mahmoud Shabistarī puts it:

اگر يك ذرّه را بر گيرى از جاى

همه عالم خلل يابد سراپاى

"If you remove a single particle out of its place, the whole world tumbles down."

b) The generalisation of the results of a limited number of experiments in the form of general laws and scientific theories becomes meaningful if the principle of causality holds. Because in accepting something as a law we also accept that:

(i) Every effect has a cause,
(ii) The relation between cause and effect is indispensable,
(iii) Similar causes entail similar effects.

In practice, no one can be sure of considering all the relevant factors and parameters. Therefore, generalizations cannot have absolute validity. This limitation, however, arises from the deficiency in our information. In any case, we believe that faith in the existence of absolute laws can be meaningful only if the principle of uniformity of nature is valid. As Planck put it:

"Of course it may be said that the law of causality is only after all a hypothesis. If it be a hypothesis, it is not a hypothesis like most of the others, but it is a fundamental hypothesis because it is the postulate which is necessary to give sense and meaning to the application of all hypo-theses in scientific research. This is because any hypothesis which indicates a definite rule presupposes the validity of the principle of causation." [171]

c) Should the principle of causality turn out to be invalid, nothing would be the result of a proof, because the proof is the cause of our knowledge of the desired result, and if the tie between proof and result is non-essential, the proof may not end in the result. In such a case nothing would be the result of a proof; and any proof might lead to any result; and there would be no difference between producing a proof and not producing it. That is why even those who reject the principle of causality accept it implicitly, because they admit that their proof will undermine our faith in the principle of causality.[172]

d) As the late philosopher Murtadā Mutahharī and the late Allāmah Mohammad Bāqir Sadr have pointed out,[173] the impossibility of prediction in atomic domain arises from our ignorance about the deterministic laws governing atomic phenomena rather than ineffectiveness of the principle of causality and its corollaries in the atomic world. This in itself is due either to the deficiency in the means of experimentation or due to the immeasurability of the effects of the experimentalist on the experiments. In any case, we should note that our failure in the discovery of a cause does not mean its non-existence, and we have no proof to say that modern science has discovered all the relevant factors. As Einstein put it:

"Therefore, the fact that in science we have to be content with an incomplete picture of the physical universe is not due to the nature of the universe itself but rather to us." [174]

and in the words of Henry Stapp:

"And contemporary quantum theory treats these events as random variables, in the sense that only their statistical weights are specified by the theory: the specific actual choice of whether this event or that event occurs is not fixed by contemporary theory.

The fact that contemporary physical theory says nothing more than this does not mean that science will always be so reticent. Many physicists of today claim to believe that it is perfectly possible, and also satisfactory, for there to be choices that simply come out of nowhere at all. I believe such a possibility to be acceptable as an expression of our present state of scientific knowledge, but that science should not rest complacently in that state: it should strive to do better. And in this striving all branches of scientific knowledge ought to be brought into play ... In this broader context the claim that choice comes out of nowhere at all should be regarded as an admission of contemporary ignorance, not as a satisfactory final word" [175]

Some scientists have even talked about the possibility of non-physical causes. In the words of the Canadian mathematician John Byl:

"Suppose for the sake of argument, that one could establish the definite absence of a physical cause in Quantum events. This still leaves open the possibility of non-physical causes. These might be human minds, spiritual beings such as angels or demons, or even the direct action of God Himself. Such non-physical causes are, by definition, beyond scientific enquiry. Thus, it is scientifically unwarranted to assert that the absence of physical cause entails the absence of any cause. [176]

In fact, it was in this spirit that David Bohm constructed a hidden variable quantum theory that is causal and can reproduce all of the experimental results of the ordinary quantum theory.

e) Those scientist who tried to explain human freedom by appealing to the breakdown of the law of causality, misunderstood the meaning of free will. It is true that we freely make decision to do this rather than that, but our decisions are based on our motivations and other causal agents.

It is interesting that all of these points that Mutahharī had mentioned in the early 1950's, were pointed out by eminent physicists like Dirac and de Broglie in the 1960's.[177] In fact, work on causal quantum mechanics has got some momentum in the last two decades and some eminent physicists like the Noble Laureate physicist G. 't Hooft are working on causal theories.

In short, the denial of the principle of causality is the denial of scientific laws as well as the negation of reasoning. Science has to accept the principle of causality with all its inseparable corollaries, in order that its existence could be meaningful.

Index of Names

A

Aaron, ...167
See also, Hārūn
Abduh, Shaikh Muhammad .101
Abraham...........94, 124, 145, 196
See also, Ibrāhīm
Adam 9, 24, 36, 37, 68, 72, 73, 111, 142, 168
'Alī, Imam 13, 65, 68, 75, 121, 132, 168, 170, 177, 180, 183, 185
Abd al-Rahman al-Kawakibi ..96
Abd al-Razzāq Nawfal 97
Abu Hamid Al-Ghazzali ..3, 4, 5, 6, 7, 9, 93, 94, 171, 172, 173, 215, 231
Abu Ishaq al-Shatibi 99
Abū Shākir Daysāni 128
Ād 178, 184
Albert Einstein...... 137, 138, 140, 198, 200, 204, 221, 222, 224
Al-Biruni 52, 53, 100, 105
Alexis Carrel, Dr. 149
al-Raghib al-Isfahani 84
Al-Shatibi 99
Al-Suyuti.................................95
al-Tantawe..............................97
al-Tusi 30, 100
Aristotle 54
Avicenna 148, 190
See also, Ibn Sina
Ayyūb 145

B

Beheshtī, Dr.............................219
Bertrand 150
Born, Max............. 200, 201, 221

C

Cardozo...................................150
CERN 35
Charles H. Townes 151
Charles Richet 151

D

David 10, 143, 144, 145
See also, Dāwūd
David Bohm 225
Dāwūd................... 143, 144, 145
Dirac...............................222, 225

E

E. F. Schumacher................88, 90
Erwin Schrödinger..................90

F

Fakhr al-Dīn Rāzī, Imam.....131, 164, 219
Fayd al-Kashani, Mulla Muhsin 6, 7
Freeman Dyson.......................88

G

G. 't Hooft................................225
Gallen......................................54
Gautama..................................151
George Sarton....................30, 52

H

Hāfiz.......................................167
Hārūn......................................145
Heisenberg, Werner...... 140, 220
Helmhotlz...............................137
Henry Stapp...........................224
Hermite...................................150

I

Ibn al-'Ukhuwwa.....................57
Ibn al-Haytham.............. 53, 100
Ibn Ikhwah........................57, 58
Ibn Mas'ūd...............................93
Ibn Sina...........30, 100, 148, 190
Ibrāhīm. 124, 145, 164, 196, 197, 197, 211, 215
See also, Abraham
Iqbal, Muhammad..................58
Īsā.................. 143, 145, 149, 220
See also, Jesus
Ishāq, *also Isaac*......................145
Ismā'il Pāshā's.......................102
Ismāīl, *also Ismael*.................145

J

Jacob......................................145
See also, Yaqūb
Ja'far al-Sādiq, Imam.........15, 38
Jalāl al-Dīn Rūmī.....60, 167, 178
Jālūt.......................................143
Jesus Christ.... 143, 145, 149, 220
See also, Īsā
Job...145
See also, Ayyūb
John Byl.................................225
Jonah.....................................145
See also, Yūnus
Joseph.................................... 120
See also, Yūsuf

K

Kekulé....................................152
Khomeini, Imam..............59, 69
Khwajah Nasir al-Din Tusi 30

L

Levy..52
Luqman...................................85

M

Mach......................................140
Mary.........................89, 143, 149
See also, Maryam
Mary Midgley..........................89

Maryam 143, 149, 220
Maurice Bucaille 98
Max Planck 137
Maxwell 204
Mohammad Bāqir Sadr 224
Moses 18, 146, 151
See also, Mūsā
Mufaddal ibn 'Umar 38
Muhammad, Prophet . 3, 26, 36, 37, 56, 60, 64, 74, 75, 78, 83, 98, 131, 169, 231
See also, Prophet
Muhammad al-Hādī 121
Mulla Sadra 7
Murtadā Mutahharī . 8, 136, 220, 224, 225
Mūsā 134, 146, 147
Mustafa Sadiq al-Rafi'ī 96

N

Nehru 81
Newton 138, 198
Noah, *also Nūh* 18, 145

P

Pharaoh 18, 180, 184
Philip Frank 140
Planck 221, 223
Prophet 5, 8, 9, 10, 11, 13, 26, 27, 36, 38, 40, 56, 60, 64, 69, 74, 75, 76, 78, 83, 96, 100, 101, 122, 131, 168, 169, 177, 180, 182, 185, 186
Popper, K 91

Q

Qurashi 84
Qutb al-Din Shirazi 30

R

Riemann 150

S

Sa'di 25, 26
Sādiq, Imam al- 40, 121, 127, 128, 132, 189
Sadr al-Dīn Shīrāzī 7, 217, 231
Sayyid Qutb 28, 62, 206
Shaikh Mahmūd Shabistarī ... 29, 222
Shaikh Mahmud Shaltut 31
Shaikh Mufīd 128
Shaikh Muhammad Bakhīt 97
Shaikh Mustafa al-Maraghī .. 102
Sir Sayyid Ahmad Khan 31
Solomon, *also Sulaymān* 10, 144, 145

T

Tantawi 31
Tabatabā'ī, Allamah S.M.H. .. 85, 104, 163, 164, 168, 171
Thamūd 178
Toulmin 87

U

Umar Khayyam 30

W

Wigner, Eugene 90

Weierstrass..............................150

Y

Yaqūb.....................................145

Yūnus 145

Yūsuf......................................120

End Notes

I. Science and the Muslim Ummah

1 Kulaynī, *al-'Usūl min al-Kāfī* (Beirut: Dār sa'b wa Dār al-Ta'āruf, 1401 H.), Vol. 1, P. 30; Ibn Mājah, *Sunam* (Damascus: Dār al-Fikr, ?), Introduction, Sec. 17, No. 224.

2 Abū Hāmid Muhammad al-Ghazzali, *'Ihyā 'Ulūm al-Dīn* (Beirut: Dār al-Ma'rifah, ?), Vol. 1, P. 14.

3 *Ibid,* p. 15.

4 *Ibid,* p. 16.

5 *Ibid,* p. 39.

6 *Ibid, p.* 22.

7 Muhsin Fayd Kāshānī, *al-Mahajjah al-Baydā fi Tahzīb al-'Ihyā* (Qum: Daftare- Inteshārāte Islāmī, ?), Vol. 1, P. 59.

8 *Ibid,* p. 71.

9 Sadr al-Dīn Shīrāzī, *Sharh 'Usūl al-Kāfī* (Tehran: Institute for Humanities and Cultural Studies, 1367), Vol. 2, P. 8.

10 *Ibid,* p. 5.

11 *Ibid,* p. 8.

12 *Ibid,* p. 39.

13 Murtadā Mutahharī, "Farīzehe 'Ilm", *Guftār-e Māh,* (Tehran: Kitāb Forūshī Sadūq, 1341 S.), Vol. 2, p. 137.

14 al-Susūtī, *al-Jami' al-Saghīr min Hadīth al-Bashīr al-Nazīr* (Damascus: Maktabah al-Halbūnī, ?), Vol. 1, P. 148.

15 Sadūq, *al-'Amālī* (Beirut: Mo'assisah al-A'lamī lel-Matbūāt, 1400 H.), p. 27.

16 Ali-Akbar al-Qurashī, *al Nizam al-Tarbawī fi al-Islam* (Beirut: ?), P. 188.

17 Zaynal-Dīn Āmilī, *Munyah al-Murīd fi Adab al-Mufid wa al-Mustafid* (Qum: Daftar-e Tablighāt-e Islāmī, 1368 S.), P. 104; al-Suyūtī, *op. cit.*, Vol. 2, P. 255.

18 Sadūq, *op. cit.*, P. 394.

19 al-Suytī, *op. cit.*, Vol. 1, P. 196.

20 *Nahj al-Balāghah*, edited by S. al-Sāleh (Beirūt: ? , 1967), P. 393.

21 Āmidī, *op. cit.*, P. 126.

22 Even in this case it may be said that the religious information of most of the Muslims is very scanty, and unfortunately most of the laws of Islam have, in practice, lost their social relevance.

23 Kulaynī, *op. cit.*, Vol. 1, P. 27.

24 Fatlāl Nayshābūrī, *Rawdah al-Wā'izīn* (Qum: Manshūrāt al-Rāzī, 1386 H.), Vol. 1, P. 12.

25 Majlisī, *op. cit.*, Vol. 1, P. 184; al-Ghazzālī, *op. cit.*, Vol. 1, P. 90.

26 Zayn al-Dīn Āmilī, *op. cit.*, PP. 101-102.

27 Zayn al-Dīn Āmilī, *op. cit.*, P. 134; Ibn Mājah, *op. cit.*, Introduction, Sec. 23, No. 258.

28 Majlisī, *op. cit.*, Vol. 2, P. 37; al-Suyūtī (With slightly different wording), *op. cit.*, Vol. 2, P. 487.

29 Zayn al-Dīn Āmilī, *op. cit.*, P. 169.

30 Sayyid Qutb, *Fi Zilāl al-Qur'an* (Beirut: Dār-o 'Ihyā al-Turāth al-Arabī, 1386 H.), Vol. 6, PP. 262-263.

31 George Sarton, *Introduction to the History of Science* (Baltimore: The Williams and Wilkins Co., 1927), Vol. 1, PP. 520-783.

32 A. Nawfal, *al-Muslimūn wa al-'Ilm al-Hadīth* (Beirut: Dār al-Kitāb al-Arabī, 1973), P. 5.

33 M. Shaltūt, *Tafsīr al-Qur'an al-Karīm* (Beirut: Dār al-Shorūq, 1981), PP. 13-14.

34 Abdus Salam, *Ideal and Realities* (Singapore: World Scientific, 1987), PP. 275-290; P.C.W. Davies, *The Force of Nature* (New York: Cambridge University Press, 1980), PP. 216-227.

II. The Significance of Physical and Biological Sciences in Islamic Perspective

35 Kulaynī, *al-'Usūl min al-Kāfi*, (Beirut: Dār Sa'b wa Dār al-Ta'āruf, 1401 H.), Vol. 1, P. 30: Ibn Mājah, Sunan, (Damascus: Dār al-Fikr, ?), Vol. 1, Introduction, Sec. 17, No. 224.

36 Abū Hāmid Muhammad al-Ghazzālī *'Ihyā' 'Ulum al-Dīn*, (Beirut: Dār al-Ma'rifah, ?), Vol. 1, P. 14; Muhammad Bāqir Majlisī, *Bihār al-Anwār*, (Beirut: Dār 'Ihya' al-Turāth al-Arabī, 1403 H.), Vol. 1, P. 180.

37 Sayyid Hasan Shīirazī, *Kalimah al-Rasūl al-A'zam*, (Beirut: Mo'asisisah al-Wafā, 1982), P. 403.

Sadūq reports that, while our Prophet ﷺ was describing the characteristics of wise men, he said:

﴿ ... لا يسأم من طلب العلم طول عمره... ﴾

"A wise man does not become tired of seeking knowledge throughout his lifetime."

Sadūq, *Kitāb al-Khisāl*, (Qum: Daftar-e Inteshārāt-e Islami, 1362 S.), Vol. 2, P. 433.

38 Kulaynī, *op. cit.*, Vol. 1, P. 32; Ibn Mājah, op. cit., under No. 233; Tarmazī, *al-Jāmī al-Sahīh* (Sunan), (Beirut: Dār 'Ihyā' al-Turāth al-Arabī ?), No. 2682.

39 al-Suyūti, *al-Jāmil' al-Saghīr min Hadīth al-Bashīr al-Nazīr*, (Damascus: Maktabah al-Halbūnī, ?), Vol. 2, P. 657; see also Majlisi (with a slightly different wording), *op. cit.*, Vol. 2, P. 16.

40 Majlisī, *Ibid.*, Vol. 3, PP. 82-83.

41 Harrāī, *Tuhaf al-'Uqūl an 'Āli al-Rasūl* (Qum: Daftar-e Inteshārāt-e Islami, 1363 S.), PP. 335-336.

42 R. Levy, *The Social Structure of Islam*, (Cambridge: Cambridge university Press, 1957), P. 460.

43 G. Sarton, *Introduction to the History of Science*, (Baltimore: The Williams & Wilkins Co., 1927), Vol. 1, P. 5.

44 Abū Rayhān al-Bīrūnī, *Kitāb Tahdīd Nihāyāt al-Amākin le-Tashih Masāfāt al-Masākin*, Persian translation by A. Ārām, (Tehran: Tehran University Press, 1352 S.), PP. 3-4.

45 Abū Rayhān al-Bīrūnī, *Kitāb al-Jamāhir fi Ma'rifah al-Jawāhir* (Hyderābād, India: Mạtba'ah Jam'iyyah Dāerat al-Ma'ārif al-'Othmāniyyah, 1355 H.), P. 5.

46 'Ibn Abī 'Usaybi'ah, *'Uyūn al-Anbā' fi Tabaqāt al-Atibbā* (Beirut: Dār Maktabah al-Hayāt, 1965), PP. 552-553.

47 Sadūq, *Kitāb man lā Yahduruh-ū al-Faqīh* (Tehran: Maktabah al-Sadūq, 1394 H.) Vol. 4, P. 334. In Bukhāri's *Sahīh* (chapter on funeral rites) this tradition is reported in a slightly different form, but with the same meaning. M. Bukhārī, *Sahīh al-Bukhārī*, (Beirut: Dār 'Ihyā' al-Turāth al-Arabī, ?)

﴿الاسلام يعلوا و لايعلى﴾

48 M.J. Mughniyah, *al-Tafsīr al-Kāshif*, (Beirut: Dār al-'Ilm lil-Malāyeen, 1968), Vol. 2, P. 465.

49 Ibn al-'Ukhuwwa, *The Ma'ālim al-Qurba fi Ahkām al-Hisab*, edited, with abstract of contents, glossary and indices by R. Levy, (London: Messrs Luzac & Co., 1938), PP. 56-57.

50 M.J. Mughniyah, *al-Fiqh alā al-Mazāhib al-Khamsah* (Beirut: Dār al-'Ilm lil-Malāyeen, 1977), P. 499.

51 Rūhollah Khomeinī, *Tahrīr al-Wasīlah*, (Qum: Daftar-e Inteshārāt-e Islamī, 1363 S.), Vol. 1, PP. 445-446.

52 Zayn al-Dīn 'Āmilī, *Munyah al-Murīd fi Adab al-Mufid wa al-Mustafid* (Qum: Daftar-e Tablighat-e Islami, 1368 S.), P. 137.

53 Sayyid Qutb, *fi Zilāl al-Qur'an*, (Beirut: Dār-o 'Ihyā' al-Turāth al-Arabī, 1386 H.), Vol. 2, PP. 560-561.

54 al-Ghazzālī, *op. cit.*, Vol. 1, P. 14; Majlisi, *op. cit.*, Vol. 1, P. 180.

55 Majlisi, *op. cit.*, Vol. 2, P. 99; al-Suyūti, *op. cit.*, Vol. 2, P. 255.

56 Majlisī, *Ibid.*, Vol. 2, P. 105.

57 'Āmidī, *Ghurar al-Hikam wa Durar al-Kalim* (Qum: Dār al-Kitāb al-Īslamī, 1410 H.), PP. 324-325.

58 Ibn Abd al-Birr al-Qurtubī, *Jami' Bayān al-Ilm wa Fadleh* (Beirut: Mo'as-sisah al-Kutub al-Thaqāfiyah, 1995), P. 122.

59 *Nahj al-Balāghah*, edited by S. al-Sāleh, (Beirut: ?, 1967), P. 219.

60 *Sahīfeh-ye Nour*, (Tehran: Sāzmān-e Madāreck-e Farhangi-e Inqelāb-e Islamī, 1361 S.), Vol. 13, P. 206.

III. Science and Ethics in the Qur'anic Outlook

61 Muslim Ibn al-Hajjaj, *Sahīh Muslim*, Vol. 3, # 1829 (Beirut: Dār 'Ihya' al-Turāth al-Arabī, 1955), P. 1459.

62 al-Suyūti, *al-Jāmi' al-Saghīr min Hadīth al-Bashīr al-Nazīr*, (Damascus: Maktabah al-Halbūnī, ?), Vol. 1, P. 558.

63 Imām Alī, *Nahj al-Balāghah*, edited by S. al-Sāleh (Beirut: ?, 1967), P. 242.

64 al-Suyūtī, J., *op. cit.*, Vol. 1, P. 185; The same tradition has been narrated by M.B. Majlisi, though with a slightly different wording: M. B. Majlisi, *Bihār al-Anwār*, (Beirut: Dār 'Ihya' al-Turāth al-Arabī, 1983), Vol. 2, P. 32.

65 al-Muttaqī, *Kanz al-'Ummāl* (Beirut: Mo'assesah al-Resālah, 1985), Vol. 3, # 5217, P. 16.

IV. From Knowledge to Wisdom: A Qur'anic Perspective

66 Honderch, T., *The Oxford Companion to Philosophy* (Oxford: Oxford University Press , 1995) , P.912.

67 Stein, J, The Random House Dictionary of English Language (New York: Random House Inc. 1973), P. 1639.

68 The Bible: Authorized King James Version, Proverbs, 2: 4-5, P. 724.

69 Majlisi, M. B., *Bihār al-Anwār* (Beirut: Dār 'Ihyā' al –Turāth al Arabī, 1983), Vol. 21 , P. 211.

70 Al-Raghib al-Isfahani , *Mufradāt al-alfāz. al-Qur'an fi Gharib al-Qur'an* (Beirut: al-Dar al-Shamiyyah, 1383 H.), P.249.

71 Qurashi, S.A. A., *Qamūs-e Qur'an* (Tehran: Dār al-Kutub al-Islāmīyah, 1352 H) , Vol. 1, P. 163.

72 Tabatabai, S. M. H. , *al-Mīzān fī Tafsīr al-Qur'an* (Beirut: Mo'as-sisah al-A'alami lil-Matbū'āt , 1393 H.), Vol. II, P. 395.

73 Popper, K., "Natural Selection and the Emergence of Mind," in *Evolutionary Epistemology, Rationality and the Sociology of Knowledge*, (eds.) Gerard Radnitzky & William W. Bartley, III (La Sall.: Open Court, 1987), P. 141.

74 Quoted in Artigas, M., *The Mind of the Universe* (Philadelphia: Templeton Foundation Press, 2000), P. 258.

75 Dyson, F., "Can Science Be Ethical", in *Christian Ethics Today*, 3, Dec., 1997, P. 12.

76 Schumacher, E. F., *A Guide for the Perplexed* (London: Jonathan Cape, 1977), P. 14.

77 Midgley, M., Wisdom, *Information and Wonder: What is knowledge for?* (London: Routledge, 1991), P. 45.

78 Schumacher, E. F., *op. cit.*, P. 129.

79 Quoted in Richardson, W. M. et. al. (eds.), *Science and the Spiritual Quest* (London: Routledge, 2002), P. 244.

80 Wilber, K., *Quantum Questions* (Shambhala: New Science Library, 1984), P. 81.

V. Scientific Dimension of the Qur'an

81 Abu Hamid al-Ghazzali, *Ihya' 'Ulūm al-Dīn* (Dār al-Ma'rifah), Vol. 1, P. 289.

82 Abu Hamid al-Ghazzali, *The Jewels of the Qur'an,*, trans. by Muhammad Abu al-Qasim (Routledge & Kegan Paul, 1983), PP. 45-48.

83 al- Suyūtī, *al-Itqān fī Ulūm al-Qur'an* (Beirut: Dār al-Ma'rifah, ?) PP. 160-164.

84 Abd al-Rahman al-Kawakibi, *Tabāyi'a al-'Istibdād* (Dār al-Qur'an al-Karim, 1373), P. 42.

85 Mustafa Sadiq al-Rafi'I, *I'jāz al-Qur'an wa al-Balāghat al-Nabawiyyah* (Dār al-Kitāb al-'Arabī), PP. 127-129.

86 Shaikh Muhammad Bakhit, *Tanbīh al-Uqūl al-Insani* (Maktabat A. Rabi'), PP. 9-10.

87 M.H. al-Dhahabī, *al-Tafsīr wal Mufassirūn*, (Dār al-Kitāb al-Hadīth), Vol. 2, P. 505.

88 Abd al-Razzaq Nawfal, *al-Qur'an wal 'Ilm al-Hadīth* (Dār al-Kitāb al-'Arabī), P. 26.

89 Maurice Bucaille, *The Bible, The Qur'an, and Science* (Crescent Publishing Co., 1978), P. 251.

90 Yusuf Muruwwah, *al-Ulūm, al-Tabī'iyyah fi al-Qur'an* (Muruwwah al-'Ilmīyyah), PP. 161-165.

91 Maghniyyah, *al-Tafsīr al-Kāshif* (Dār al-'Ilm lil-Malayīn), Vol. 4, P. 173.

92 M.H. al-Dhahabī, *op. cit.*, Vol. 2, PP. 485-489.

93 Muhammad 'Ammārah, *al-Islam wa Qadāya al-'Asr* (Dār al-Wahdah), P. 75.

94 M.H. al-Dhahabī, *op. cit.*, Vol. 2, P. 519.

95 A. Tabārah, *Ruh al-Dīn al-'Islamī* (Dār al-'Ilm lil-Malayīn), P. 270.

96 M.H. Tabataba'i, *The Qur'an in Islam* (Islamic Propagation Organization), P. 96.

VI. Philosophy of Science: A Qur'anic Approach

97 M. H. Tabātabā'ī, *al-Mīzān fī Tafsīr al-Qur'an*, (Beirut: Mo'as-sisah al-A'lamī lil-Matbū'āt, 1973), Vol. 2, P. 360.

98 Kulaynī, *al-'Usūl min al-Kāfī*, (Beirut: Dār Sa'b wa Dār al-Ta'āruf, 1401 H.), Vol. 2, P.34.

99 Harrānī, *Tuhaf al-'Uqūl an 'Āli al-Rasūl*, (Qum: Daftar-e Inteshārāt-e Islamī, 1363 S.), P. 47.

100 al-Rāghib al-Isfahānī, *Mufradāt al-alfāz al-Qur'an fī Gharib al-Qur'an*, (Beirut: al-Dār al-Shāmiyyah, 1383 H.), P. 249.

101 Sadr al-Dīn Shīrāzī, *al-Hikmah al-Mota'āliyah fī al-Asfār al-Aqliyyah al-Arba'ah*, (Beirut: Dār 'Ihyā' al-Turāth al-Arabī (1981), Vol. 3, P.516.

102 Kulaynī, *op. cit.*, Vol. 1, P. 29.

103 Muhammad Mufīd, *al-'Irshād, fī Ma'rifah Hojajillah alā al-'Ibād* (Tehran: Inteshārāt-e Elmiyyeh Islamiyeh, ?), P . 281.

104 M. Bāqir Majlisī, *Bihār al-Anwār*, (Beirut: Dār 'Ihyā' al-Turāth al-Arabī, 1983), Vol. 3, PP. 146-147.

105 Ali Muttaqī al-Hindī, *Kanz al-'Ummāl, fī Sunan al-Aqwāl wa al-Afāl*

(Beirut: Mo'as-sisah al-Risālah, 1405 H.), No. 1220.

106 Fakhr al-Dīn Rāzī, *al-Tafsīr al-Kabīr*, (Beirut: Dār 'Ihyā ' al-Turāth al-Arabī, ?), Vol. 17, P. 209.

107 Of course, if somebody wants to refer to the analysis of what has been seen (or heard) as the eyes (or ears) of heart, we won't argue with him against his terminology.

108 *Nahj al-Balāghah*, edited by S. al-Sāleh, (Beirut: ?, 1967), P. 213.

109 M. Bāqir Majlisī, *op. cit.*, Vol. 3, PP. 159-169.

110 Abul-Hasan Nadwī, *Islam and the World*, (Malaysia, 1401 A.H.), P. 95; Muhammad Iqbāl, *The Reconstruction of Religious Thought In Islam*, (Lahore: Sh. Muhammad Ashraf, 1960), PP. 127-131; A. Tabbārah, *Ruh al-Dīn al-Islamī*, (Beirut: Dār al-'Ilm lil-Malāyeen, 1982), P. 270.

111 M. Mutahharī, *'Ilal-e Garāyesh bi Māddigarī*, (Tehran: Hekmat Pub., 1357 S.), P. 191.

112 Albert Einstein, *Ideas and Opinions*, translated by Sonja Bargamann, (New York: Donanza Books, ?), P. 270.

113 Max Planck, *The New Science*, (U.S.A.: Meridian Books, 1959), PP. 43-44.

114 Albert Einstein, *op. cit.*, PP. 273-274.

115 Werner Heisenberg, *Physics and Beyond*, (New York: Harper Torch Books, 1972), P. 63.

116 Philipp Frank, *Einstein: His Life and Times*, trans. by George Rosen, (New York: Alfred A. Knopf, 1972), P. 216.

117 Sadr al-Dīn Shīrāzī, *op. cit.*, Vol. 3, P. 384.

118 M. H. Tabātabā'ī, *op. cit.*, Vol. 16, P. 10.

119 al-Rāghib al-Isfahāni, *op. cit.*, P. 249; Samīh Ātif al-zayn, *Majma' al-Bayān al-Hadīth*, (Beirut: Dār al-Kitāb al-lubnānī, 1980), PP. 912-914.

120 M. J. Mughniyah, *al-Tafsīr al-Kāshif*, (Beirut: Dār al-'Ilm lil-Malāyeen, 1970), Vol. 6, P. 53.

121 Ibn Sīnā (Avicenna), *al-'Ishārāt wa al-Tanbīhāt*, (Beirut: Mo'as-sisah al No'mān lil-Tabā'ah wa al-Nashr, 1413 H.), Vol. 2, PP. 393-394; Sadr al-Dīn Shīrāzī, *op. cit.*, Vol. 3. P. 387.

122 Ibn Sīnā, *Ibid.*, PP. 388-391.

123 *Ibid.*, PP. 394-395.

124 Alexis Carrel, *Man, the Unknown*, (NewYork: Macfadden Publications, 1961), PP. 85-86.

125 C. H. Townes, "The Convergence of Science and Religion," *Zygon*, Vol. 1, No. 3, 1966, P. 307.

126 M. H. Tabātabā'ī, *op. cit.*, Vol. 7, PP. 289-290.

127 *Ibid.*, Vol. 8, P. 348.

128 M. J. Mughniyah, *op. cit.*, Vol. 3, P. 213.

129 Ahmad Rahsepār, *Dīn-e Arkān-e Tabī'at*, (Tehran: Kānoon-e Inteshārāt-e Sharīf, [1357 S.]), P. 251.

130 Abū Hāmid Muhammad al-Ghazzali, *op. cit.*, Vol. 3, P. 15. Sadr al-Dīn Shīrāzī, *op. cit.*, Vol. 8, P. 304.

131 Fakhr al-Dīn Rāzī, *op. cit.*, Vol. 13, P. 43.

132 M. H. Tabātabā'ī, *op. cit.*, Vol. 5, P. 270.

133 Abū Hāmid Muhammad al-Ghazzali, *op. cit.*, Vol. 3, P. 9; Muhsin Fayd Kāshānī, *al-Mahajjah al-Baidā' fī Tahzīb al-'Ihyā'*, (Qum: Daftar-e Inteshārāt-e Islamī, ?), Vol. 2, P. 125.

134 'Āmidī, *Ghurar al-Hakim wa Durar al-Kalim*, (Qum: Dāral-Kitā b al-Islamī, 1410 H.), P. 651.

135 Kulaynī, *op. cit.*, Vol. 2, P. 263. For other versions of the same tradition, see also Bukhārī, *Sahīh al-Bukhārī*, (Beirut: Dār 'Ihyā' al-Turāth al-Arabī, ?), Vol. 8, P. 105, and M. Fayd Kāshānī, *Kalimāt Maknūnah min `Ulūm 'Ahl al-Hikmah wa al-Ma'rifah* (Tehran: Inteshārāt-e Farāhānī, 1360 S.), P. 113.

136 Sadūq, *'Uyūn Akhbār al-Ridā* (Tehran: Inteshārāt-e Jahān, ?), Vol. 2, P. 69. For other versions of this tradition see, e.g., al-Suyūtī, *al-Jāmi' al-Saghīr min Hadīth al-Bashīr al-Nazīr* (Damascus: Maktabah al-Halbūnī, ?) Vol. 2, P. 483, and Fayd Kāshānī, *op. cit.*, P. 247.

137 *Nahj al-Balāghah*, *op. cit.*, P. 337.

138 *Ibid.*, P. 497.

139 M. H. Tabātabā'ī, *op. cit.*, Vol. 2, P. 250.

140 Abū Hāmid M. al-Ghazzālī, *op. cit.*, Vol. 3, PP. 12-14.

141 Sadūq, *Kitāb al-Khisāl*, (Qum: Daftar-e Inteshārāt-e Islamī, 1362 S.), Vol. 1.1, P. 51.

142 'Āmidī , *op. cit.*, P. 27.

143 *Nahj al-Balāghah*, *op. cit.*, P. 524.

144 Ibn Abī Jumhūr, *Awālī al-La'ālī al-Aziziyah fī al-Ahādīth al-Dīniyah*, (Qum: Mujtabā Arāqi, 1403 H.), Vol. 1, P. 290; see also al-Suyūtī, *op. cit.*, Vol. 1, P. 500 (for a different wording of the same *hadith*).

145 *Nahj al-Balāghah*, *op. cit.*, P. 160.

146 *Ibid.*, P. 503.

147 Sadūq, *Kitāb al-Khisāl*, *op. cit.*, Vol. 1, P. 85; for a slightly different

wording see: al-Suyūtī, *op. cit.*, Vol. 1, P. 469.

148 'Āmidī , *op. cit.*, P. 44.

149 Barqī, *Kitāb Thawāb al-A'māl min al-Mahāsin*, (Qum: Dāral-Kutub al-Islamiyah, ?), Vol. 1, P. 215.

150 'Āmidī , *op. cit.*, P. 52.

151 I. M. B. Majlisī, *op. cit.*, Vol. 2, P. 116.

152 Sadūq, *al-Amālī*, (Beirut: Mo'as-sisah al-A'lamī lil-matbū'āt, 1400 H.), P. 343.

153 Ibn Sīnā (Avicenna), *op. cit.*, Vol. 4, PP. 159-160.

154 M. H. Tabātabā'ī, *op. cit.*, Vol. 16, P. 167.

155 M. Born, *The Born-Einstein letters*, translated by Irene Born, (London: Macmillan, 1971), P. 91.

156 *Ibid.*, P. 149.

157 Albert Einstein, *Ibid.*, P. 266.

158 M. H. Tabātabā'ī, *op. cit.*, Vol. 1, PP. 45-46.

159 Sayyid Qutb, *fī Zilāl al-Qur'an*, (Beirut: Dār 'Ihyā' al-Turāth al-Arabī, 1386 H.), Vol. 1, P. 40.

160 M. Mutahhari, *Majmu'e Āthār-6* (Tehran: Inteshārāt-e Sadrā, 1373 S.), PP. 651-653.

161 Abū Hāmid Muhammad al-Ghazzālī, *Tahāfut al-Falāsifah*, (Cairo: Dār al-Ma'ārif bi-Missr, 1972), PP. 239-240.

162 M. H. Tabātabā'ī, *op. cit.*, Vol. 7, P. 298.

163 Sadr al-Dīn Shīrāzī, *op. cit.*, Vol. 6, PP. 371-372.

164 Fakhr al-Dīn Rāzī, *op. cit.*, Vol. 2, PP. 110-111; Vol. 14, PP. 193-195;

Vol. 30, P. 53; Sadr al-Din Shīrāzi, *op. cit.*, Vol. 9, PP. 153-158.

165 M. H. Beheshtī, "Qānūn-e Elliyyat dar Dīn wa Dānesh-e Basharī," *Goftār-e Māh*, (Tehran: Kitāb-forūshi Sadūq, 1341 S.), Vol. 3, PP. 114-115.

166 Murtadā Mutahharī, *'Adl-e 'Ilāhī*, (Qum: Daftar-e Inteshārāt-e Islamī, 1361 S.), PP. 114-115.

167 I. A. Einstein, *op. cit.*, P. 276.

168 Born, *op. cit.*, P. 82.

169 Ismā'īl R. al-Fārūqī, "The Causal and Telic Nature of the Universe," *Proceedings of the International Conference on Science in Islamic Polity*, (Islamabad: Nov. 1983), P.X; K. Hadring, "Causality Then and Now: Al Ghazzāli and Quantum Theory," *The American Journal of Islamic Social Sciences*, Vol. 10, No. 2 (1993), PP. 165-177.

170 G. Holton, "Einstein's Scientific Program: The Formative Years," *Some Strangeness in the Proportion*, Edited by Harry Woolf (Massachusetts: Addison - Wesley Publication Co., 1980), P. 65.

171 Max Planck, *op. cit.*, P. 104.

172 Ibn Rushd (Averroes), *Tahāfut al-Tahāfut*, translated by S. Van Den Bergh (London: 1978) PP. 316-319; M. Bāqir Sadr, *Falsafatunā* (Beirut, 1400 H.), PP. 308-309; M. Mutahharī *Majmū'-e Āthār-e*, *op. cit.*, P. 685.

173 M. Mutahharī, *Ibid.*, P. 686; M. Bāqir Sadr, *Ibid.*, PP. 314-315.

174 Max Planck, *op. cit.*, P. x.

175 H.P. Stapp, *Mind, Matter, and Quantum Mechanics* (New York: Springer-Verlag, 1993), P. 216.

176 J. Byl, "Indeterminancy, Divine Action and Human Freedom", *Science and Christian Belief*, 15, No. 2, Oct. 2003.

177 M. Golshani, "Cosmology in the Islamic Outlook and in Modern Cosmology", in N.H. Gregersen, U. Gorman & H. Meisinger (eds.), *Studies in Science & Theology*, Vol. 8 (Aarhus: University of Aarhus, 2002), PP. 187-188.

www.ingramcontent.com/pod-product-compliance
Ingram Content Group UK Ltd.
Pitfield, Milton Keynes, MK11 3LW, UK
UKHW012253290726
14090UKWH00016B/630

9 789671 037911